*The*

# Sweet Potato Queens'
# Field Guide to Men

*Every Man I Love Is Either*
*Married, Gay, or Dead*

ALSO BY

*Jill Conner Browne*

The Sweet Potato Queens' Book of Love

God Save the Sweet Potato Queens

The Sweet Potato Queens' Big~Ass Cookbook
(and Financial Planner)

# The Sweet Potato Queens' Field Guide to Men

## Every Man I Love Is Either Married, Gay, or Dead

### Jill Conner Browne

 THREE RIVERS PRESS • NEW YORK

Grateful acknowledgment is made to Zamalama Music Publishing, Inc., and OF Music, Inc., for permission to reprint an excerpt from "Every Man I Love Is Either Married, Gay, or Dead" written by Sharyn Lane and Rich Fagan. Copyright © 2000 by Zamalama Music Publishing, Inc. (BMI)/OF Music, Inc. (ASCAP)/administered by Bradley Music Management, Inc. Recorded by Kacey Jones for IGO Records on the CD titled *Every Man I Love Is Either Married, Gay, or Dead*. Available at www.KaceyJones.com or (877) 999-9975. Reprinted by permission of Bradley Music Management, Inc.

Published by Three Rivers Press, New York, New York.
Member of the Crown Publishing Group, a division of Random House, Inc.
www.crownpublishing.com

Three Rivers Press is a registered trademark and the Three Rivers Press colophon is a trademark of Random House, Inc.

Sweet Potato Queens® is a registered trademark of Jill Conner Browne. The Sweet Potato Queens® characters, names, titles, logos, and all related indicia are trademarks of Jill Conner Browne and/or SPQ, Inc.

Printed in the United States of America

*Design by Lynne Amft*
*Photographs by Tom Joynt, copyright © 2003 by SPQ, Inc.*

Library of Congress Cataloging-in-Publication Data
Browne, Jill Conner.
The Sweet Potato Queens' field guide to men : every man I love is either married, gay, or dead / Jill Conner Browne.—1st ed.
1. Men—Humor.   2. Man-woman relationships—Humor.   I. Title.
PN6231.M45B65      2004
818'.5407—dc22          2004006305

ISBN 1-4000-4968-7

10   9   8   7   6   5   4   3   2

First Edition

For my sweet mama, *Janice Wendt Conner,*
who taught me the joys of reading and eating
(especially at the same time) and who provided me with
the best daddy the world has ever known.

And for my beloved sister, *Judy Conner Palmer,*
who shared my idyllic childhood and has, to this very day,
somehow resisted smothering me in my sleep.

# CONTENTS

# Contents

## Contents

# Contents

*The*

# Sweet Potato Queens'
# Field Guide to Men

*Every Man I Love Is Either
Married, Gay, or Dead*

# *Getting Started*

## *Every Man I Love Is Either Married, Gay, or Dead*

If being a mother is like being pecked to death by a duck (and don't we all know *that's* true?), then being a wife or girlfriend or somebody's significant other must be more like—well, what *is* it like? How best to describe this relationship? As so often happens when I come up against a tough question, my thoughts turn to Daddy and his stock of growing-up stories. And as usual, Daddy came through.

As a young man, Daddy used to visit a certain bootlegger's establishment in Attala County, Mississippi. (Since Mississippi was legally dry until 1968, everybody knew the local bootlegger and where to find him.) The bootlegger's wife had a medium-sized monkey that she kept as a pet and doted on like it was blood kin. One day, when Daddy happened by to make a purchase—for medicinal purposes only, I imagine—Mr. Bootlegger was nowhere to be found, but Mrs. Bootlegger shouted through the screen door that Daddy should come on in and she'd help him.

No sooner had Daddy crossed the threshold than something dropped from the sky—actually, the sill above the door—and landed with a very loud shriek, its little grabby hands and feet on the back of Daddy's young and tender neck. With no thought or planning whatsoever, Daddy reached up and back, grasping whatever it was and flinging it as hard and fast as he could against the far wall. The first time he actually saw his assailant was when it landed *smack* against the wall in a sort of plastered-out, spread-eagle position. Then it slid silently down the wall, leaving a pitiful trail of urine to mark its descent. It was, of course, the monkey.

Well, needless to say, much weeping and wailing and gnashing of teeth ensued—from Mrs. Bootlegger and also from the monkey as soon as he roused himself. Daddy thought it best to flee the premises posthaste, without pressing further his own desire for a drink (although, truth be told, the incident had considerably heightened the urge).

What, you may well ask, does this have to do with the issue at hand—that being relationships between women and men? Over the course of my own personal love life, I have played the role of the innocent and unsuspecting one, bounding goofily along, happily trusting that all was right with the universe, and fully expecting all my needs and desires to be fulfilled, only to be blindsided by something singularly unpleasant and often life-altering—the metaphorical flying monkey, if you will. I've even been the monkey, too, once or twice. In childlike exuberance, I have dropped unbidden and unwelcome into a situation and found myself whizzing through the air, smashing into the wall, and landing with a thud on the floor in a befouled heap of my own emotions. With no small degree of shame, I must also admit to putting myself—maybe without malice but certainly not without aforethought—into situations I had no business being in and, karma being what it is, received the much-deserved wall-flinging and then some. I've even been the innocent wall, merely standing by in the wrong place, with bad timing, too, when I've been suddenly hit with the flying monkey messes of someone else's creation. And who hasn't been Mrs. Bootlegger, forced to watch in helpless horror as those you love play out some hideous scenario that you know can have no happy ending?

Love gone bad is at least interesting, if only in a macabre sort of way. It's surely not boring. Love gone *blah* is simply death—slow, torturous, and ultimately longed-for death. When you're mired in a lifeless, life-stifling, life-smothering relationship, you start to take it for granted. Life sucks, always did, always will, and so you're just hunkered down, *enduring* this relationship. As far as I know, nobody is handing out prizes, tangible or other-wise, for endurance of life its ownself. In my experience, if you ignore your life, it will pretty much ignore you right back. I reckon the universe figures why should it bother sending you anything else if you haven't got any more gumption than that.

Prizes are handed out in a continuous stream, however, to folks committed to *living*. When you finally wake up and look around, you realize that your life has been so bad for so long, it's no longer even painful to you. And when you get yourself up on your hind legs and take action, you'll not only wonder *how* you stood your misery for so long, but you will ask that all-important question, *Why?* Why did you bear that burden for so long when apparently you were wearing the Ruby Slippers the whole time? It doesn't really matter too much why—as long as you start clicking those heels together and devote a fair amount of time each day to grinning and looking around you.

But what are you looking for? What are we all looking for? If it's love, the city animal pound is full of creatures literally dying to love you, and you can have all you can fit in your car anytime you want. No, it's not just love we crave. We're looking for another *person* to love and, equally important, to be loved by. One without the other just sucks—as in, shit through a straw. And we can all testify ad nauseam to that, but no one has voiced our agony better than Kacey Jones, the Official Songstress to the Sweet Potato Queens, when she recorded "Every Man I Love Is Either Married, Gay, or Dead." Kacey sings many songs that perfectly describe many aspects of our lives, but we consider this one to be our anthem. (Go now to sweetpotatoqueens.com to get your very own copy.)

## Getting Started

Now, we happen to be heterosexual female types, through no fault of or credit to ourselves—it's just the way we turned out, which is the way these things *do* happen, by the way. As such, we find that we, personally, are most interested in loving and being loved by heterosexual male types, and thus we refer in this book almost entirely to this particular branch of humankind. We are fairly sure, however, that the hoops we all jump through in the dance of love are pretty much the same, regardless of our orientation, and so we trust that you will instinctively make the necessary mental adjustments to the characters described herein. I mean, we all have to get ready to go to the dance and find a suitable partner when we get there. It doesn't really much matter who's dancing or how or with whom, now does it?

Okay, so we're going to say here that the first step is to find the guy—the one who makes your heart beat a bit faster, your breath come a bit quicker, your knees wobble, your hands tremble, your mouth water, and—the ultimate test of True Love (or, at the very least, Lust) at First Sight—the one who can *make you lose your appetite*. Omigod—this is the Holy Grail of Guys. I wish I could find one of these a *month*, but I don't have to tell you they are scarce as hens' teeth. (That expression has always intrigued me, on account of it implies that roosters *do* have teeth. It doesn't say "scarce as chickens' teeth"; it specifically singles out the *hens* as the ones being toothless. And then it always makes me think how funny chickens of both genders would look if they actually did have teeth. And then I think about the boyfriend of a friend who resembles nothing quite so much as a chicken with teeth, and by now you can see why it's a good thing that I don't have a real job, because this is really and truly the kind of stuff I think about all day long, no matter what it is that I'm actually *supposed* to be doing.)

Okay, so we've got to find the guy. Where to look? Well, hunny, open your eyes. We are just covered up in guys. Seriously, they are absolutely everywhere. If you were a dead-cat-slinging kinda gal (though I sincerely hope you're not), you simply could not do it without hitting multiple guys at every sling. (Where do these sayings come from? It's maddening, I swear.) If you're looking to buy china, do you go to the hardware store? Likewise in relationships. If you want an intellectual, quit going to tractor pulls. If you don't want to date a barfly, why aren't you at the opera? Married guys are not your best bet if you're looking for a long-term commitment. Decide what you want and then weed out all those who don't fit.

To aid you in this process, we offer *The Sweet Potato Queens' Field Guide to Men*. Believing, as we do, that you are just like us, we will identify and classify for your edification and enjoyment as many different variations on the Man theme as we can think of and some of the potential pitfalls inherent in them. We hope this will help you decide what you want, even if it's by discovering what you don't want so that you end up with the right thing by default. When my good friend Janice Wright learned about this book, she heard the title spoken, rather than saw it written, and the question that immediately popped into her

somewhat-less-than-virginal mind was "Did she say *field* guide
or *feel* guide?" And what an excellent question that is! We purely
love to feel men—some more than others, obviously.

One of our precious Wannabes went with us once to a body-
building competition. We were carrying on in our customary
fashion (loud), and after climbing down off our chairs for a
moment, we noticed that she was not joining in either our chair-
standing or our caterwauling. Rather, she was sitting and gazing
with rapt attention, hands clasped in an almost prayerful fashion beneath her quivering little chin, her breath coming in pant-
like fashion in and out of her mouth, which could best be
described as agape (not to be confused with *agape*). "What's the
deal?" we asked her. She turned her nearly teary eyes to us and
in a faint whisper said, "I . . . never . . . knew . . . never . . .
saw . . . never . . . dreamed. Omigod! Who knew a man's body
could look like that?!" We said, uh, well, yeah—DUH! "I can't
imagine what all that *feels* like!" she gasped. And again, our
snappy rejoinder was something along the lines of "Uh, well,
yeah, DUH!"

And then she literally burst into tears. "I just close my eyes
and tell myself," she whimpered, " 'This is a *good* man, this is a
*sweet* man, this is a *decent human being*,' over and over. And then
I just try real hard not to touch anything squishy." Oh, dear, we
thought, those are not egg-zackly what you'd call words of lust,
and we just hoped to God she never said any of them out loud
anywhere else—say, in the tepid of the moment, as it were.
"Shins and elbows," she said. We must have looked mystified

because she went on to explain that those were his body parts she tried to focus on—everything else was pretty much guaranteed to squish if touched. I confess to having a near fetish about hands and forearms—I find them wildly attractive—but never have I given a moment's thought to shins and elbows. I'm not sure it would do much for me, can't really imagine that it would, and it didn't seem to do much for our friend, either. She sniveled through the entire show, but she was pretty successful at stifling any outright sobbing.

I wonder if maybe her husband was firmer when they first met, fell in love, and married, and then went squishy later on or if she knew the job was squishy when she took it. For any guys who've wandered off in this book in search of guidance, be advised: We are not really much into squishy; if we were, we'd date women. We generally prefer that your entire body feel completely different from our own, not just that one part, although that particular part is certainly important to us. Also, we really do like to be the only one of the two of us who's got tits (here again, if we wanted that, we know plenty of women). At any rate, I think it's a good idea to give a guy a pretty good prenup feel before you haul off and marry him; you don't want any surprise squishiness sneaking up on you postnup.

Feeling of men in general—just for sport—is highly entertaining for us, and for them, too, we find. We have discovered that, while in the gym, you can walk right up to a guy with a fabulous body and ask if you can feel of him and his face will just light right up. (I'd suggest doing this in groups of at least two. You run the risk of creating a less-than-desirable impression if you do it solo, and besides, guys love an audience as much as we do.) First, we survey the crop available at any given time for a while and we try to reach a consensus on who we should feel of first. This gives us something fun to ponder while exercising, and you know how time does fly when you're looking at hot guys. Then we'll pick one and walk right up to him and ask if he minds if we just feel of him for a minute. I can tell you we have never been denied access. And then we just rub his big, muscular arms and carry on as if we were Meg Ryan in *When Harry Met Sally*. The more we feel, and the longer and louder we moan and groan and giggle, the more teeth he shows. This is one guy who will not be slacking off on his workouts anytime soon. And it gives the rest of 'em a little boost, too—makes them all work just a little bit harder in hopes of being our chosen Feelee the next time around.

So, in answer to Janice's question—yes, it's a feel guide *and* a field guide to men. It is also an excellent guide *for* men. Men can learn a lot here if they pay attention. (The Cutest Boy in the World calls our books "manuals on how to get laid.") We hope all will benefit from the Sweet Potato Queens' many years of experience in affairs of the heart, loins, mind, and tummy. This tells you there will be love, lust, lessons, and food, too, up in here. Come on in, hunny.

## PART I

# Common Varieties and Habitats

# 1

# Typical American Specimens

We will pretty much be discussing American men, since they're the kind we know best, but certain similarities are bound to exist internationally. We present eight of the most common specimens of the American adult male. This is by no means an exhaustive list, but we believe we have identified and classified those men who are the most highly evolved, as well as those who, in our opinion, are way down the evolutionary ladder. You will have no problem figuring out which is which. In fact, you may be familiar with men who fit two or more of the categories simultaneously.

Certain general types will be identified along with their physical characteristics; at the same time, common variations of the type will be identified as well. The scientific category for these specimens, as determined by the Sweet Potato Queens, is Spud. Measurements are included for some Spuds, and these are given in feet and inches, pounds and ounces. (We considered adding the metric equivalents in parentheses for anybody who cares but quickly decided that nobody does, so we're not.) Height refers to the measurement taken from the top of the skull (hair, if it exists, real or make-believe, will not be considered for this purpose) to the sole of the foot (with the heel resting firmly on the ground—no tippy-toes allowed).

Also included where pertinent will be information regarding Habitat. Where a Spud is spotted may offer important clues as to his identification, much as the tree squirrel will always be found in wooded areas and prairie dogs are pretty much gonna be out on the wide-open grasslands. Although location or Habitat of some types is specific to certain regions, this is usually not the case. In our experience, you can find assholes pretty much everywhere.

Any particularly important attributes will be shown in *italics. Habits* will tell you the time, day or night, when the man is most active and what he's likely to be up to then. When known, information will be provided on nesting, food, longevity, breeding season, and other habitual practices that may be of interest. Information on the *young* may be included where relevant. The *economic status* refers to the man's ability to Pay for Things and, more important, his willingness to do so. *Longevity* is greatly influenced by the subject's habits, particularly in the *nesting* and *breeding* subcategories.

Some of these Spuds are considered to be *poisonous* and extremely *dangerous,* and we wish there were some consistent pattern of distinguishing physical characteristics (like pointy heads or red and yellow stripes or big fangs) we could share with you so that you could RUN AWAY! RUN AWAY! whenever one is spotted in your vicinity. Unfortunately, however, no thoroughly reliable profile exists. As we said before, assholes are everywhere, and many of them have developed elaborate systems of camouflage that make them difficult to detect. We do hope to offer some assistance in your screening process.

The Ultimate Man identified by the Sweet Potato Queens is the Spud Stud, and there is no similar breed. He is IT, and our studies indicate that the Spud Stud is the only variety of Spuds currently on the endangered species list. There are many other varieties out there, though. And best we wade through them first since they will be the most *plentiful* and readily *available.* The reader should not infer any degree of fairness intended by these descriptions; they are used purely for the sake of conversation and, we hope, for laughs. It is not in my job description to be fair to men or to even *seem* fair to them. It's a little late in the history of the entire world to introduce an element of *fairness,* and beyond even my considerable powers to bring it to bear, anyway. So, fine. Occasionally, the universe has a brain fart and something fair randomly happens. For instance, our good friend Irv got prostate cancer. No, that's not the good part; even we aren't *that* mean, for goodness' sake. We love Irv *and* his prostate. But anyway, Irv's a physician, and so, of course, he went for two years before going in to seek actual treatment for this condition—typical guy, typical guy M.D.—and of course, the condition had worsened considerably during the interim.

Once he finally went for treatment, among the things his doctors did was to put him on a massive regimen of hormones— *our* kind—to suppress all of *his* kind, which they hoped would slow the growth of the cancer. So what I'm telling you here is this: They dropkicked ole Irv's ass smack into the middle of menopause! And they've told him he'll be on this regimen for two years. Yes, ma'am, I am here to tell you, a bunch of us were at our favorite restaurant—Bravo!—here in Jackson, Mississippi, sipping ever-so-daintily on our ReVirginators and nibbling deli- cately on a big platter of their special Sweet Potato (Queen) Fries, when Irv all of a sudden breaks into a major sweat and starts fanning away at his hot little self. We were yelling at him that he was cooling off the fries, man, and he launched into his tale of 'Pause Woes. Hunny, you woulda thought you were at a baby shower listening to Ida Faye and Bertile expounding on the Change. Irv said he was plagued night and day with these hot flashes of the *severest* order. (Of course, if it's happening to a *man*, it's the worst thing that ever happened to anybody in the history of the world, and nobody could possibly understand or even imagine how terrible it is.) He spoke of finding himself standing in front of the open freezer, trying to cool off, and then, as long as he was there, eating gobs of ice cream straight out of the carton, and he hadn't even been hungry a minute before.

Irv also described enormous swings of mood, being giddy as a carload of sixth-grade girls at the mall one minute and madder'n a frog with a firecracker up its butt the next and then sad—ohhhh, just so, so *sad*—and all for no apparent reason that he could tell. He described bursting into tears in the checkout line at the grocery store when he realized he didn't have his SuperSaver card with him and he was not going to be eligible for the big discount on his 'tater chips and Co-Colas. Now, he was telling us all this with a completely straight face—except for when his lip quivered and his eyes kinda filled up. I reckon he was expecting that we would, like, *sympathize* with him or something.

We dutifully listened without interrupting until he got to the part about crying in the grocery store, and then we all kinda looked at each other and just lost it simultaneously and completely. We were howling and high-fiving and banging on the table and generally having a high old time at the total expense of the hapless Irv. Lucky for us, this was not one of his weepy times—or pissed-off times—and he took it pretty well. When we finally calmed down, he said that the hormone experience had really given him a better understanding of women—as a physician. Said he had treated women patients his entire medical career and he had *never believed a word* of the symptoms they described until now, when they were happening to him, his very ownself. *Now* he gets it. Of course, now he's retired, so he can't put it to use in his practice, where it might benefit *us*, but we're just happy that there is currently on the planet at least one man who has a deep, personal understanding of What It's Like.

We'd like to see a law passed that requires all straight men to take at least a year's worth of hormones—and try to just "get over it" and "deal." Oh, yeah, baby—show us what you got *then!* And men who plan to become ob-gyns—they must take the hormones throughout their entire course in med school. Now we're talking "fair." (On the flip side, though, we do have that multiple-orgasm thing going.)

So in the interest of "fairness" and to show that we don't take ourselves too seriously, in the pages to come we'll also examine a few female types—we call them Yams—who might be expected to pair off with certain Spuds.

## The Bud Spud

Also known as the "boy friend," the Bud Spud can and will serve in many capacities and meet many of our needs—all but one, truth be told. Bud Spuds can be talked to, they can be danced with, they can often fix things, and they are more than welcome to pay for things. But we do not have sex with them except on very rare occasions that most often involve dim lighting and too much alcohol. A very wise person once said, "Never fuck your friends," and I'm sure they meant that literally and figuratively. Words to live by.

## Typical American Specimens

The *measurements* of the Bud Spud are completely irrelevant except in some cases for dancing. Some women don't like to dance with the Short (just as some men don't like to dance with the Tall), but me, I don't care since I never slow-dance anyway, so it doesn't matter to me a-tall. If your Bud Spud is on the hefty side, you can be assured not only of eating well but, perhaps of equal importance, of eating happily. I positively *loathe* eating with people of any kind who do not love food, don't you? I think I speak for all the Sweet Potato Queens worldwide when I say, "We are not afraid to eat." I do not necessarily loathe the food-apathetic people themselves (although I wouldn't rule it out), but I simply will not eat with them if I can avoid it, even if it means going hungry for a spell my ownself.

When we were in Los Angeles, shooting the pilot for a Sweet Potato Queens sitcom at the Warner Bros. Studios, we found we were something of a freak show at our many and frequent restaurant meals. This would be primarily because of our breathtaking beauty, you are no doubt assuming, and you're right, of course, but it was *also* because we actually eat food. No one who lives in Los Angeles ever actually *eats*—at least not in public, where they might be *seen* or even photographed for the scandal sheets. And believe me, eating in L.A. is scandalizing to the locals. They hardly ever order anything but salad—the lettuce brokers in L.A. must live like kings is all I'm saying. And everybody orders everything "on the side"—the dressing, naturally, *if* they even allow it in their presence. If there happen to be any other items included in the salad that could possibly possess a shred of a calorie, those items are either deleted or requested "on the side," where they can be picked at with a fork and looked at with a mixture of suspicion and disdain, if not outright disgust. We saw diners recoil in horror from proffered baskets brimming with beautiful breads. You would have thought the waiter was attempting to put a bucket of turds or snakes or snake turds on their table (one of my favorite ex-husbands used to describe an extreme case of intoxication as being "snake turds drunk," and though I never fully grasped the concept, I did gather that it was pretty damn drunk). It did give us pause to wonder exactly how these folks would react to something truly shocking or appalling.

One of our very favorite eateries is Kate Mantellini's on Wilshire Boulevard. The menu is so large as to be initially daunting, but we soon discovered that any fears we might have were groundless because everything on the menu is just about the best thing you ever ate in your *en*-tire life, and we know this because we ordered everything on the menu just about every time we ate there, which was nearly every day for a week. You don't really have to worry about making "the right choice"—you can safely just close your eyes and point to something, and you'll be happy with it, I promise. I love that about a restaurant. Nothing quite pisses me off as much as bad food; even if I didn't have to cook it myself, I'm *still* hungry.

There was a big giant group of us, to be sure—me and the Cutest Boy in the World and Tammy Carol and Tammy Donna and Tammy Cynthia, our precious darlin' George, our captive computer guy, Jay, and our most beloved buddies, Katie Dezember and Dennis Black—so we would always get the big giant booth by the window and we would also get all the attention. The waiters flocked to our table, chattering excitedly with us. (Waiters in L.A. are not generally found to be "chatty." It's as if the prospect of eating is so mortifying for both the servers and the diners alike that everyone concerned just tries to pretend it's not happening. This is much like the attitude adopted by medical professionals and us during pelvic exams. Everybody just talks about the weather and pretends they are not actually down there under a sheet, up to their eyeballs and elbows in *you*.) But once the waiters got over their initial shock that not only were we going to *order* a whole shitload of actual food—with nothing "on the side" unless it was additional sauce, dressing, or gravy—but we were actually going to *eat* it—all of it—plus massive quantities of wine and hard liquor and dessert—well, now, I can't rightly say that they ever did truly get over it, but at least when they came to, they were just positively giddy with excitement. I don't know who was more excited: us at the prospect of consuming the sumptuous repast, or the entire staff of the restaurant at the prospect of getting to watch us do it. Some folks do just purely love to watch, don't you know.

So anyway, we love to eat and we love our friends who love to eat, be they Queens or Bud Spuds. Exercise some caution when eating for entertainment, however, lest you become a Ham Yam.

Your Bud Spud can be of just about any sexual orientation you can think of—and it seems to me there are a lot more choices these days than there used to be. It really doesn't matter how he likes it—it ain't gon' be happenin' with *you*, so what do you care? His hands and feet can look like little monkey hands and cloven hooves as long as they are fully dedicated to your service.

His *habitat* is likewise of little importance unless you are likely to end up sharing it with him, and it is entirely possible—in many cases highly desirable—to share living quarters with one's Bud Spud. As long as you have your own bathroom (bedroom goes without saying) and he has a good cleaning lady, it should work out just fine.

The *young:* If he does have offspring for whom he is personally and financially responsible, we would hope that he tends to them in his off-hours, when he is *not* tending to you and your needs. Of course, the ideal situation is for him to be a complete and total orphan, with no living relatives of any kind anywhere. He should, on the other hand, be wildly entertained by the very prospect of spending time, energy, and money on any offspring that *you* personally happen to have. But, of course, a Bud Spud truly worthy of the name will be completely entranced by any and every thing connected in the slightest way to you and your life.

A really good Bud Spud will be so completely happy in his devotion to you that he will just live forever—and mercy, I hope so, since it will be close to impossible to replace him. The thought of nearly anyone's death is unpleasant, to be sure (do

note that I said "nearly" anyone's, as there are, of course, excep-
tions), but the thought of our own demise and that of our nearest and dearest is troubling indeed. It would be best all around
for *us* if we were to die first, though. I mean, if we depart first,
our Bud Spud will grieve in a very gratifying manner and see to
it that we are remembered fondly and sent off in grand fashion.
If he precedes us in death, we will be expected to do all those
things for him and he won't be here to help us: Our lying-down
days will be over until we do, in fact, go off to lie down permanently, and then he won't be here to handle our funeralizing. If
he has an ounce of human decency, he will not die first. No, it
makes much more sense in the long run to take very good care
of our Bud Spuds and make sure they live very long lives. Just
in case, though, it's always a good idea to have a spare. A veritable stable of Bud Spuds would make one sleep better at night,
I should think.

I personally have a precious Bud Spud who received a wind-
fall of cash from an unexplained but apparently felicitous source
and decided, unaided, that he wanted to buy me a very fine
watch. Not being in possession of a very fine watch, I was naturally amenable to this. We went to the very fine watch store
and narrowed the field down to two choices—both very fine
and very expensive, but one appreciably more so than the other.
He had me try them both on repeatedly and finally said, "Well,
you can have either one you want, but I'm just telling you right
out, if you get *this* one"—indicating the wildly expensive
model—"you are just gonna have to put out." Whereupon I

snatched up the other one and told the salesman, "This 'un'll do just fine, thankee." And we were all happy.

If you're lucky enough to have a really good Bud Spud, you must take extreme care to protect his delicate feelings. You walk a fine line with him: You know he absolutely love-loves you—and you love him only as a Bud Spud. You must be very careful not to imply by word or deed that you harbor any deeper feelings for him or that there's any chance in this lifetime that you will develop deeper feelings for him. You must force yourself to be completely honest with him, even though this is really hard, because you don't want to hurt his feelings and you wish you did love-love him, and if you had any sense, you probably would love-love him, but you don't. If you lead him on and let him think otherwise, you are guilty of being a Flimflam Yam, and you will be punished. As a matter of fact, if you mess around and break his heart—and he happens to be a Bud Spud of *ours* as well—we will call you a Damn Yam. And when we get through with you, you'll know you've been set upon by the Wham Yams.

## The Dud Spud

The Dud Spud, as his moniker clearly states, is . . . well, he just fails to meet our expectations or requirements in some critical way. The particular critical way is intensely personal, however, and one woman's Dud could be the next woman's Stud. This is a good thing, and because of this diversity in taste and needs, hardly any Spuds need ever be completely relegated to the waste heap. The Dud is not a bad sort at all; he's just not what we had in mind. We most often encounter the Dud Spud on blind dates: Your girlfriend has *the* most fabulous guy in the world and she cannot wait for the two of you to meet. He's perfect, she's swearing. Let's say you have a height preference in your men and you make inquiries regarding this *measurement,* and she oohs and aahs about how very tall he is and you fall for it. Upon introduction, you see that, yes, in fact, he does positively tower over your friend, but then, you note, *she* is only four-eleven. Dogs and a whole lot of fourth graders tower over her. For future reference, short people have no perspective on height—not only does everybody look tall to them, everybody *is* tall.

My good friend Catherine (The Great, naturally) shared with me a detailed accounting of the Dud Spud experiences that she has endured—at the hands of friends. Granted, there are assorted strokes for assorted folks, but I find it hard to imagine that these guys show up in anybody's fantasy. I don't know if she changed their names before she told me about them, but I'm changing them now, just in case—although I feel fairly certain none of them can actually read.

Jim was described as being "tall with silver wavy hair." He was five feet ten, and the top six inches of that was an astounding gray pompadour. Nobody could have prepared Catherine for his showing up in a lime-green leisure suit with matching patent-leather shoes (mmm—not just green but shiny, too) and a green-and-yellow tie. The only vehicle he owned was a fishing boat.

Gilbert could have been cute, if he had not been allowed to dress himself. Yeah. Cheap shoes and more jewelry than a Waffle House waitress. Cheap shoes are a deal-killer for so many of us. Catherine opined that you could tell a lot by a man's shoes, and she did not mean the size of the shoes, either. As an added bonus, he was the worst kisser since junior high, according to Catherine, and the way she described it intrigued me; I would love to watch him do it. She said he just stuck his hard, pointy tongue smack in her mouth and then moved his head around—not his tongue. One of those things that just begs the question: What was he thinking?

Chad was a doctor (Gasp! A doctah! She threw back a doctah?) who was benched after one date during which he had ordered chicken but sent it back to the kitchen to be deboned so he wouldn't have to get his fingers messy. Waaaay too prissy and no doubt there was some foreshadowing of his attitudes toward sex, don't you imagine?

Bob's pick for a lunch meeting? Denny's—and then he paid with coupons and asked her to leave the tip. But even Bob was better than the next guy, who doesn't even rate a fake name—let's just call him Tightwad, or Wad for short. Wad took her to her favorite restaurant, but when the check came, he snatched it up and said, Well, she had wine and he didn't, so her portion of the bill was _____, whereupon our intrepid Catherine smiled like the Queen she is and said, "Oh, you know, why don't you just let *me* buy dinner tonight," and of course, that was just fine by him. She tipped big, and she and the waitress exchanged knowing glances—as in "We know he's goin' home by himself!" Oh, but wait! It gets better. Wad actually had the nerve to call and ask her out again, and she just lied and said her old boyfriend had made a comeback appearance, and he got all huffy and said, "Well, I only wish I had known *that* was on the horizon before I invested so much emotional time in you!" I guess he *was* emotional over losing a woman he didn't have to invest any money in.

Catherine said at one point she thought a certain Gary had potential. He asked to meet in a snazzy place; he was there waiting when she arrived, and he was not only handsome, he was perfect. Truth be told, the more she looked at him, the more overwhelming the state of his absolute perfection became. He appeared to have been professionally groomed and styled for the occasion, and you know we cannot stand for a guy to spend that much time in front of a mirror, but he was good-looking and polite and he was paying for the date and she was trying to talk herself into overlooking this big red flag that read NARCISSIST sticking out of the top of his head. Then he came by the house and her teenage daughter took one look at him, fled, and called Catherine into her room, where she was in a fetal position on her bed, laughing hysterically into a pillow. Coming up for air, she delivered his death knell in a shrill whisper: "He looks just like a game show host!" And she was *right*, of course—for two hundred dollars! As Catherine was saying good night to him a few minutes later, her daughter passed by, and out of the mouth of this babe came the faint sound of the theme from *Jeopardy!*

Then Catherine had the ultimate blind date: He was actually *blind*. This would have been fine had anybody bothered to mention that salient fact to her beforehand. I mean, how could you forget to tell somebody her date is blind? Not that she would have refused to go out with him, but she might have prevented some awkward moments, such as when the *realization* hit her and when he realized that the realization was hitting her. They got past it, naturally, but she couldn't help thinking she had put on makeup for nothing.

A final note: Women who are subjected to an overly large number of Dud Spud encounters may get trigger-happy with the front door in their haste to get rid of the Duds. These women are known as Slam Yams.

## The Crud Spud

The Crud Spud's *measurements* are *not* important. There is no physical attribute he can possess that is powerful enough juju to overcome his inherent, well, cruddiness. Many levels and variations of Crud exist, but not a one of them is acceptable. Queen Monica from Wisconsin wrote that, for her birthday, her Crud Spud gave her a bottle of his favorite men's cologne—for *him* to wear, but for *her* pleasure. Please! Maybe he thought this was like when we buy trashy lingerie to wear for them. But it is *so not* the same thing at all. First of all, she was not looking longingly at the stinky men's cologne ads in the magazine, and she most certainly was not scratching and sniffing the pages and begging him to "git summa dis, baby." She thought she had outgrown having to be around guys bathed in rancid cologne way back in the sixties, after the Great Jade East/English Leather Stink-Off was held among all the seventh-grade boys in the United States. It's a pretty fair indicator of this guy's own self-absorption that he didn't even know that she hated the smell of it, and we won't even talk about the thought process that led him to buy *himself* a present for *her* birthday. He was completely blindsided, of course, by her total lack of enthusiasm for his "gift": How could she not be positively corybantic at the very thought of an olfactory experience involving *him?* He was still wearing that puzzled expression the last time she saw him— which was when she closed the door.

That is Crud Spudism at its mildest. But, you know, if you don't nip the bud of Crud, it will only fester and flourish. Remember that guy who was in the Army, stationed overseas, and it came to light that more than *fifty* women thought they were engaged to him—at the same time? He had met most of them on-line and just wooed away with all of them, and one thing would naturally lead to another, as it so often does, and next thing you know, there'd be an "engagement," and the two of them fixing to get married. He got caught when one of the chosen fifty was interviewed in her local newspaper, and she spoke glowingly of her "fiancé," who was off protecting us all in the foreign fields. Well, a wire service picked up the story, and in no time at all, there was just a whole big ole pile of pissed-off women, each thinking she was the One. And of course, none of 'em was the One. They were all "another" one, just like the other ones. Whooo-ee! There were forevermore some mad women, and they wanted the Army to do something about it. Seems to me the best thing the Army could do was just ship him home and let the fiancées know when and where his plane was landing. They were in bad need of some satisfaction.

Queen Leesa wrote to tell me the Crud Spud experience of her dear friend Annabelle, who had the great misfortune of being wedded to Hideous Roy. When he wanted his groom's cake to be Ding Dongs, she should have known that disaster was on its way. Suffice it to say, the whole marriage—or in this case, shooting match—was over in a matter of months, and she considered herself—and rightly so—well rid of his sorry ass. But when he announced that he loved another and planned to marry the poor, blighted individual on the very day that would have been his and Annabelle's first anniversary—well, something just snapped and Annabelle vowed revenge.

Annabelle ranted and she raved—and who wouldn't have? —threatening deeds ranging from arson to zip guns and including everything in between, and believe me, there's a *lot* in between, and he did so richly deserve all of it. Annabelle was in such a tizzy that Leesa and their dear friend Bonnie became convinced that if they didn't intervene quickly, a close encounter with a bail bondsman was in Annabelle's immediate future. They knew they couldn't just tie her up and wait for it to pass;

this would *never* pass. They would have to offer an alternative—and nothing with poison in it.

So what they did was, they went to the big local department store together, with Annabelle posing as the newly anointed Mrs. Hideous Roy-to-Be and Leesa and Bonnie posing as her maids of honor, and they proceeded to register the happy couple for each and every butt-ugly item they could find in the store. The chosen gifts included painted faux-porcelain figurines (usually described in catalogs as "lifelike resin," meaning "plastic"), cheap floral dishes with plaid tablecloths of clashing hues, bath towels with appliquéd swans, sheets very low in the thread count but very high in the polyester count, scores of useless appliances, and all manner of awful stemware and cutlery. There was so much icky stuff to choose from, it was very difficult to narrow down their selections. (Isn't it fun to shop for others?) And then, just to add to their own personal pleasure at their plot, the address they gave for shipping and delivery belonged to the mother of Hideous Roy, who had been less than cordial to our dear Annabelle during her short tenure as Mrs. Hideous Roy. Their happiness was nearly complete.

On the actual weekend of the erstwhile first anniversary/second wedding, Bonnie and Leesa had a Queenly gathering for Annabelle to celebrate the brevity of her stint as Mrs. Hideous Roy. Annabelle volunteered to bring the dessert. Of course, she showed up with a white bakery box containing the top of her wedding cake—which they ate down to the last crumb, thankyouverymuch.

Queen Delta Dawn learned, through many painful years of dating, that when a guy tells you he's a jerk and that you shouldn't date him, believe him: He is a jerk, and you shouldn't date him. A guy told her that once, and she thought he was just "being cute." She compounded this wrongheaded thinking with the belief that she could change him. Do we even have to say it? *Wrong!* Fortunately, Delta Dawn had a Bud Spud who 'splained some things to her. Regarding the self-described jerk, Bud Spud wisely asked who knows him better than he knows himself? Regarding change, Bud Spud assured her that an asshole will remain an asshole until *he* gets tired of it. Until then, there's nothing anybody should do but get away from him. Happily, Delta Dawn listened to the wise counsel of her Bud Spud and learned how to pick a *good* guy the next time, and she's been blissfully married to him for a bunch of years, with plans for a bunch more.

There are a few *habits* up with which I will not put—eating or actively chewing gum while talking to me on the telephone, for instance. How is it, in our current technological age, that there are apparently some humans who're unaware that a telephone receiver acts as an amplifier, and that consuming foodstuffs no more substantive than pudding, and having it amplified through a telephone and spit into someone's ear, sounds exactly like—well, it sounds like somebody spitting in your ear, and it is *maddening* and not a little nauseating. I have had people eat *carrots* on the phone with me—although not for very long. I've been known to simply hang up and later claim "dropped call." My shiny new husband, the Cutest Boy in the World, said that he broke up with a girl once because she smacked her food when she ate. He actually *told* her that was why he was breaking up with her, which makes me cringe in horror for her—can you imagine? She vowed she would stop, but he held firm, believing that if she had gotten to the fully growed stage still smacking like a dog with a mouthful of peanut butter, then she was probably pretty much committed to it. I definitely would have broken up with a guy for the same offense, but I'd never have had the nerve to actually tell him the real reason—I woulda prolly told him I'd decided to take up with women or join the Peace Corps or something. (Come to think of it, I did go out with a guy once who asked everybody at the dinner table, "Are you gonna eat your fat?" As I said, I only went out with him once, so I didn't have to explain table etiquette to him.)

Those habits are giant red flags whipping in the wind, but the *habitat* of the Crud Spud can be just as telling. If you should, for some inexplicable reason, find yourself in the place he calls home, and you are there by your own volition—meaning you have not been drugged and hog-tied and you can therefore get up and move about the premises freely—then by all means do so, and *pay attention* as you do. My friend Frannie was invited to drop by the Habitat of a new Spud once. He greeted her at the door with a full-body embrace accompanied by a tonsil-tickling kiss that propelled the two of them toward the sofa within mere seconds. Careening backward, trying simultaneously not to stumble and bite his tongue off while looking around through eyes that appeared to be passionately closed but were really just squinted to allow for surveying the premises, she felt her dread-and-doom barometer was about to explode. She could not spot a single, solitary surface in the room not covered by multiple and varied levels of papers, dirty clothes, old pizza boxes, half-empty beer bottles, overflowing ashtrays, and cat hair.

Upon touchdown on the sofa, her senses were assaulted by one of the foulest aromas known to the human nose. She knew instantly what it was and that it was close by—*very* close by— and indeed, she was not mistaken in this presumption. When he retracted his tongue from her esophagus and began, with great enthusiasm and spectacular sound effects, to show his desire and intention to relocate his attentions to her various other body parts, she seized upon a nanosecond to turn her head just ever so slightly to one side and there it was, just as she suspected, only much closer than even she had allowed herself to believe. Right by her ear and slightly above her shoulder was a steaming pile of cat shit!

Now, had she stayed another—oh, if his time out of the gate was any indicator, another three to five minutes would have been more than sufficient—she could have taken his *measurements* and maybe found he was hung like a mule. But there's no force on earth more powerful than cat shit, and that's just a fact. And so she very quickly extricated herself from his embrace and left him and his measurements languishing in perpetual mystery. She had all the information she needed.

———

As you can see, some of these Crud Spudisms are admittedly worse than others. They range from offputting personal habits to narcissism as a vocation to the truly trashy, but it's pointless to linger in any relationship thinking you can *change* a person. People never change into something different; they just get more the *same*, and we have to extrapolate that if a little bit of it is bad, a whole bunch more of it will really suck.

When dealing with a Crud Spud, it's best to develop a slick, Teflon-like psyche and let his cruddiness just slide right off. Think of yourself as a duck's back, and don't for a minute even allow yourself to *consider* running over one of them in your car—as much as some of them deserve it and as entertaining as it would admittedly be. Be a Pam Yam, not a Ram Yam, and just slide on out the door.

## The Fuddy-Dud Spud

The *habitat* and the *habits* of the Fuddy-Dud Spud tell his whole tale. Okay, this picture should sum him up: He's obsessively neat about his person, his abode, his office space, his vehicle. He won't even leave the house to get the Sunday papers without taking a shower, shaving, fixing his hair, and donning perfectly pressed jeans. (Of course, just the very idea that he fixes his hair is enough to tear it for me personally.) He has a dining room with actual dining room furniture, and he keeps the table fully set with china, crystal, and silver—all the time. He does this himself—no help from even a housekeeper—because nobody else could do it to suit him. His desk is scrupulously neat—a place for everything, everything in its place, and heaven help you if you touch anything on it. His car, an eight- to ten-year-old Japanese compact, besides being sanitized, has a bumper sticker that says IT'S HARD TO BE HUMBLE WHEN YOU OWN A CHIHUAHUA. Doesn't it go without saying that he's single? And single he should remain. The Fuddy-Dud Spud is clearly a waste of our time. There is absolutely nothing about him in need of our woman's touch; he is more woman than *we* are interested in being—and he's an old woman at that!

If you are also obsessively neat and very prim and proper, if you like everything to be just so, and if you hold certain rules to live by in a lock-grip—like, for example, "Only whores have pierced ears"—then you could be our mother. You'll probably be very happy with the Fuddy-Dud, and we'll just call you Ma'am Yam. If, on the other hand, you've found yourself a Fuddy-Dud who makes you happy, Chihuahua notwithstanding, and you can perk him up—get him to kick it up a notch, as it were (with a nod to Emeril)—you'll go down in history as a Bam Yam.

## The Pud Spud

We-e-e-ll, I'm not really sure if the Pud Spud is necessarily a *bad* guy, but I do believe there's something awry in his wiring. The Pud Spud is not an Olympic swimmer, he is not a professional cliff-diver, nor is he an Ironman Triathlete. Yet he wears a Speedo swimsuit and apparently he does so without qualm one. And, for the record, let me just say that even if he is an Olympic swimmer, professional cliff-diver, and the reigning champeen of Ironman Triathlons—unless he's in the very middle of doing one or all of those activities right this very minute—he does not need to be poolside in his little bikini panties. Talk about off-putting. I personally could never take a man seriously who wears a Speedo in public (not that I'd be any happier about him wearing one in private). I'd always be going, "What the hell is he thinking?" and I would never get a satisfactory answer—there simply isn't one—except that maybe he wants to attract other men, in which case, fine by me. Next!

One of my daddy's favorite jokes was about the three guys going to the beach. One is a major stallion and his two buddies are, well, they're a cross between a Shetland pony and a dumb-ass. The stallion is going to the beach every day in his little Speedo, and the women are following him around, wagging big time, while the two ponies have only each other's company to keep. They beg him for his secret, and he relents and tells them that he puts a potato in his swimsuit before he goes out. So they can't wait to try it the next day, and they do. But after a day at the beach in their new accessories, they come in that afternoon, crestfallen and alone. They berate the stallion for giving them false information; they had had absolutely no luck at all attracting women. And as they left the room, their problem became apparent: They had put the potato in the back.

I did hear from one Queen—she lives in Texas and that's *all*

I'm telling—who said she personally had once had a fairly satisfactory close encounter with a Speedoed man. It seems that Queenie was lolling on the beach with a fellow Queen in Isla Mujeres—a fine lolling place, by the way—when she happened to cast her gaze toward the water and glimpsed what could have been an oversized Idaho severely taxing every fiber of the Speedo into which it had been stuffed. Queenie elbowed her girlfriend and said, "We-ell, looky THE-ERE!" And with that she promptly trotted out to the water and commenced to "drown." The rest, as they say, is—well, it's the best part, but decorum prevents further discussion.

Okay, so that was one isolated incident involving a positive interaction between a woman and a Speedo. Don't bank on it, is all I'm saying. While I'm at it, let me also say that if you are a guy and you plan on taking your clothes off in front of us, we'd really prefer that you wear some cute little boxer shorts. We really do hate tighty-whiteys—all of us, each and every one. I have never in my life met a woman who liked them, not ever, not one. And no, it doesn't help if you buy them in colors; everything about them is repulsive, not just the color. We may not openly complain to you about how gross we think they are, but you should not mistake this polite silence for genuine appreciation. We're just pretending not to notice—like if you had a big booger whistling in your nostril.

If you are a guy and you just loooove your little white man panties, then you should know that we believe they are in the same class as our own beloved granny panties. In other words, wear them when you're flying solo. We will wear pretty little panties if *you're* gonna be seeing 'em, and you, please, return the favor by investing in some big-boy underwear to wear for *our* viewing pleasure. And if you really do think we like men's bikini briefs, you've been watching too many porn flicks.

## The Blood Spud

The Blood Spud is also known as the Man Who May Need Killing. This is the Spud most likely to end up in a newspaper article about somebody getting beaten to death with a shoe, or sewed up in the bedsheets and beaten with broom handles, or accidentally run over nine times by a Hummer and that was only because she couldn't put her hands on an actual tank. (Until recently I thought that the taking up of one's shoes to club to death one's significant other was a purely Southern fancy. To the contrary, the practice is apparently sweeping the country, and small wonder: It must be so satisfying. I read in the newspaper recently that a woman in Brooklyn, New York, caught her boyfriend out at a restaurant with another woman, and that just tore it for her. After she expressed her extreme displeasure with him, he responded by punching her in the mouth and knocking out her two front teeth. Well, that was a mistake. She weighed in at 220—and she got him down, sat on his chest, and clubbed him slap to death with her size-twelve high-heeled shoe. Hard to work up much sympathy for him; he had to know the job was dangerous when he took it.)

One of my former husbands worked for a true Blood Spud once. At a business dinner, with several employees' wives there (although the boss's own wife was notably absent), this guy actually said out loud and in my presence these very words: "I never fuck anybody uglier than my wife." That has to rank in the Top Three Worst Things Ever Uttered by a Man. Someone stood up and expressed surprise and doubt that he ever got that close to any woman—was that *me?* Ahhh, yeah, and probably the only thing that kept me from advising his poor wife of his high standards was my erstwhile husband's promise to quit that job the very next day. Even though I never told this scuz bucket's wife (although I'm sure it wouldn't have come as an earth-shattering shock to her, since, after all, she did live with him), I do wish I'd told his mama. Don't you know she would have been proud?

That very same Queen who so graciously shared her Speedo success story with us also had occasion once upon a time to be lawfully wedded to a bona fide Blood Spud. Queenie had all the responsibility for their three kids, plus she worked all day in the salon she owned. According to him, however, she did nothing right at home and she didn't make enough money. Constant verbal and physical abuse convinced her that she *was* worthless and couldn't leave him, and even if she did, no other man would have her. Excuse me, she's a gorgeous, talented, hardworking, sweet-talking business owner with three precious children, and nobody but this asshole would want her? That he could even utter the words is bad enough, but that she could be beaten into believing it is wretched. Such is the nature of abuse.

# Typical American Specimens

But our Queenie was reading a *Woman's Day* magazine one day, and she came across an ad for Cameo Lingerie, which described their home party plan and how she could make a shit-load (her words, not Cameo's) of money while working part-time. She looked into it and decided to give it a try. Well, she ended up with twenty women working for her and that first year made around a hundred grand, as she says, "selling lingerie to country women." Queenie wrote me, "Give a country girl a chance to become a lingerie model in her friend's home, and you will get rich. Believe me." She was the number one director for the company that year and won a trip to Hawaii with the other top producers. She was so excited, until King Asshole announced that she would *not* be going on that trip or any other.

Queenie was devastated, but the turn of the worm had begun. She secretly packed a suitcase and hid it at a friend's home. The night before her great escape, perhaps sensing the change in her, her husband beat her severely enough to quell any possibility of rebellion, or so he thought. Despite him—and *to* spite him—she left the next day and flew to Hawaii. As soon as she got off the plane and looked at the sun setting over the ocean and the palm trees gracefully stirred by the gentle breeze that was kissing her bruised face, the calm beauty of it all overwhelmed her. She just stood there and bawled. At that moment she realized, If I am smart enough to get myself to a place like this, then I am smart enough to leave that rotten sonofabitch when I get home. She pranced her little ass right up to the car-rental booth and presented her credit card (obtained without his knowledge or—gasp, worse!—his permission), and she rented herself the fastest, reddest Corvette convertible they had. She was *living* for the first time in years. The day she came home, she packed up her kids and left. And with that, dear readers, Fifi was born—to the delight and joy of anybody who's ever visited the Queens' message board at sweetpotatoqueens.com. Let the church say "Amen."

And we are all so lucky that she didn't just haul off and kill his sorry ass, much as he deserved it, on account of we might never have met her if she had. Even in Louisiana they will sometimes put you in jail if you kill one. We've stated repeatedly that we are unequivocally against killin' 'em, even when they practically *beg* for it by their every word and deed. If you do, you will miss quite a few St. Paddy's parades in Jackson while running from the law, and you'll be a Yam on the Lam.

Since Fifi prudently did not kill the SOB and was therefore free to move about the country, she moved herself and her babies off to Texas, and a few years later a true Prince Charming came by in his sailboat and whisked her away and they are living happily ever after. Now, before she found him, Fifi had quite a number of Mr. Wrongs—so many, in fact, she had sorta stopped looking. By and by, her precious baby girl went off to cheerleading camp, and her first day there one of the other girls yelled out at the group, "Hey, who's got a cute single mom?" And Misti yelled, "I do! I do!" They compared photos and decided they both had really cute parents and wouldn't it be fun to fix 'em up? And they tried and they tried and they could not make it happen. They even convinced Paul (the cute dad) to call Fifi up and ask her out—repeatedly—and she just would not go. So one day, he just showed up at a school function where Fifi was hauling in something like six hundred hand-decorated cupcakes, and having spent so much time decorating cupcakes, she hadn't put a speck of decoration on her face, which for a Texas girl is worse than being buckass nekkid in the middle of the freeway. But when he finally got to meet her in person, in spite of her best efforts to the contrary, it was pretty much love at first cupcake. Awwww.

I love the image of Fifi and the truckload of cupcakes—this girl will go to some trouble for things. Let me just tell you what else she did. One year she was planning to head over to Jackson from Texas for our parade (Mal's St. Paddy's Parade, third weekend of every March—come on down) and she wanted to bring a little somethin' to all her buddies on the SPQ Message Board of Love. She thought and she thought and finally she hit on it: Jell-O shots! And the crazy woman made six hundred Jell-O shots and hauled them all over here in coolers. She called the hotel on the way and told them that "a number of the ladies in my party are diabetic, and we will be needing refrigerators in our rooms for the insulin." The hotel sent the fridges, and she filled 'em up with Jell-O shots. It's well within the bounds of safety, I think, to say that a good time was had by all. We do love us some Fifi. How many ways can one woman be a role model?

Speaking of role models, Queen Robin confided in me that around the time her fourth husband was divorcing her for his twenty-eight-year-old secretary, she knew she was facing a major blue Christmas a few months down the road, so she booked a Santy Claus cruise for herself and her kids. As luck would have it, along about Thanksgiving, she met a precious darlin' *twenty-six-year-old* boy. So, feeling truly thankful, she decided he could probably do with a little sea air and sunshine as well, and she invited him along on the cruise. He had his own cabin and he cheerfully played by her rules—no contact when she was with her kids—but they all had a very merry Christmas, and she charged the whole thing—including the boy toy's vacation—to the soon-to-be-ex-husband's Visa card. Such a merry little ho ho ho!

There are a lot of misconceptions floating around about aging, the top one being "It won't happen to me." Ha! Hide and watch, buckwheat. It'll happen, all right, and much sooner than you can possibly imagine. Another wrongheaded notion is thinking that, just because the *outside* of us changes, we also change on the *inside*. Wrong. People don't change—they get more and more the same. I saw in the paper that an eighty-three-year-old woman got her old self thrown in the slammer for stabbing her husband to death. He was ninety-five! A psychiatrist quoted in the article expressed the professional opinion that aging doesn't necessarily make someone a better person. Apparently not— that guy'd had *ninety-five years* to get better, and he did not use his time wisely. (Bless her heart, she just could not wait another minute for him to die.) The old woman was placed among the general female population at the jail and was evidently quite the favorite among the inmates: The jailer reported that the other women were all helping her out any way they could. That is the sweetest story. Don't we all hope that if we find ourselves newly incarcerated when we're nearly a hundred, the other girls will be nice to us?

Queen Evelyn sent me an article from the Covington, Louisiana, newspaper about one poor woman who was so upset about a mess her husband had made, she availed herself of a last resort–type measure, setting his mattress on fire. Really, sometimes there's not but one thing left to do—and haven't we all been there?—and so she just did it. Makes perfect sense to me. Well, then, once the fire got going, the two of them took turns hotly (ha-ha) insisting that the other one put it out. Finally, the fire got just too hot, and he *got out of bed*—and the two of them put it out. Now, can you believe the guy was lying there in a burning bed, hollering at her to put it out? And then, to add insult to injury, they put *her* in jail! Bless her heart, bless her poor little heart. Queen Evelyn remarked that, in her opinion (and of course she's right), if they had sent a woman officer to the scene, she would have jerked a knot in *his* ass for causing his poor wife such distress and hauled *him* off to jail for a night or two. She woulda made him clean up that mess first too. Sigh. Justice can be so elusive.

Again, it's just best *not* to actually kill your Blood Spud, but if you simply cannot resist—or if by some brilliant stroke of luck he just ups and obligingly dies of his own free will—make certain that you don't get one of those upright tombstones. They are impossible to dance on. You want one that sits flush with the ground. They're just perfect—you can even wear your tap shoes!

The Scud Spud is a veritable explosion of powerful male pul-
chritude, and you are blown away by his physical appearance.
This guy is just over-the-top good-looking. In fact, the Scud
Spud is *so* good-looking, you almost can't stand to look at him.
A hundred years ago, when I worked at the YMCA, it was covered up in gorgeous men all the time, but they were all pretty
much just regular gorgeous—you know, enough to make you
real happy to look at 'em but not enough to make you jumpy,
or as we like to say, "nervolous." (People used to ask me why I
worked at the Y *M* instead of the Y *W*, and I'm, like, ah, that
would be on account of the *M*'s, you igmo!) Then one day this
astounding specimen of masculinity walked in the front door
and joined up. I was in the office with my coworkers looking out
the big, giant one-way windows as he crossed the parking lot,
and suffice it to say, we had noticed him coming. Then we were
all jammed up in the office, peering out through a crack in the
door, watching him sign his membership papers, waiting to
pounce on the guy-employee who had taken his application and
extract from him the name of that big ole sack o' diamonds that
had just become a Y-man.

   As soon as Hercules (not his real name) left the desk and
started down the hall toward the locker rooms, we hurtled out
the door, snatched the membership papers away from the desk
guy, and learned that the vision's name was Jim. "Jim," we
sighed, and we watched, transfixed, as he sauntered down the

hall. We began to slowly creep out from behind the desk, eyes glued to his retreating back, our breath coming shorter and shorter. Making a cursory attempt at nonchalance, we steered a course toward the water fountain, and about that time, Herc peeled off his tight T-shirt, revealing more magnificence than we were prepared to witness in person on a random Wednesday. As I recall, Debbie ran smack into the wall, I gasped, "Omigod, he's *naked!*" and Alice, who was pretending to drink at the fountain, squirted water up her nose and jerked back so hard she hit her head on the top of the fountain and dang near knocked herself unconscious on the spot. Desk Guy was blowing Pepsi out his nose, he was laughing so hard.

Of course, fate being the cruel bitch she often is, we soon discovered that while he was inordinately blessed in the physical realm, many other things in life had eluded the handsome Hercules. These would include such feats as forming complete sentences, doing simple arithmetic, and breathing with his mouth closed. An intimate moment with this guy would be like staring into the eyes of a chicken. The Scud Spud would come under the heading of "All that meat—and no potatoes," and it would be accompanied by a wistful sigh.

## The Spud Stud

Also known as Mr. Right or the One, the Spud Stud is the object of our desire and the sole reason for our search. If you're really lucky and the stars align in your favor (and blind good fortune cannot be overemphasized), the clouds of confusion will part, and standing there in the sunlight of complete clarity, smack in front of you—usually with no effort on your part—there he will be, the One Who Is Just Right for You, your very own version of the Spud Stud. And what a mercy it is that "just right" has a different meaning for each of us.

*Measurements:* The height of a Spud Stud varies from knee-high to flat-footed slam-dunker and is generally thought to be irrelevant. It should be noted, however, that only specimens actually measuring over five feet nine may be trusted to give an accurate accounting of their own height. No man currently living has ever copped to being anything under five-nine, so if height is a personal requirement for you and he says he's five-nine, he's actually five-five. There are several ways to deal with a disparity in height, ranging from placing yourself on a lower step to my personal favorite, lying down. I recommend that you never throw back short specimens, at least until all other measurements have been taken, on account of *you just never know.* Weight is also highly variable, and all ranges are thought to be acceptable, although we generally prefer his weight to be noticeably greater than our own. Regarding hands and feet, much has been inferred throughout the ages from these measurements, and although the size may on occasion be relative to that of other areas, too often this is not true, and it's best not to count on it. Other comparisons aside, I personally prefer the hands and feet to look like boy hands and boy feet and to be generally larger and furrier than my own. If we are, for some reason, playing a duet on the piano, I want the casual observer to be able to discern clearly whose hands are whose. And I'm not interested in sharing shoes with any men I know.

*Habitat:* The Spud Stud is not restricted to any particular territory or area of the earth—thank *God*. Like the tree squirrel, he may be found in wooded areas, or like the prairie dog, in wide-open grasslands. He is free ranging and just as likely to show up in Noo York City as New Iberia. When you are lucky enough to find and acquire your own personal Spud Stud, you should restrict his habitat by any means available to you (from pies to Promises) to keep him close to home.

*The Young:* The offspring of the Spud Stud always receive Good Home training, and you can take them anywhere without fear of how they're gonna act when you get there.

*Habits:* The Spud Stud is likely to be active any time of the day or night—according to whatever need *you* request that he attend to in a prompt and cheerful manner. His diet is varied and interesting. Extremes in any dietary area could be grounds for demotion to a lower classification. Take, for example, vegans or, just as irritating, guys who are over forty and still won't eat their vegetables. (I dated a guy once *very* briefly, on account of the only "vegetable" he would eat—seriously—was corn.) The Spud Stud can bring home the bacon, and even if he can't actually fry it up in the pan, he knows a drive-through window where someone can. The Spud Stud has only one nest—and you're in it. Multi-nesting *demands* demotion, possibly to something in the six-feet-under category. (One of our very dear friends was really and truly married to a real, live bigamist. He was a traveling salesman, and it turned out he had wives in a whole bunch of towns. The authorities gave him serious jail time for it, and I don't think he got to keep a single wife, either. 'Course, they prolly just put him in jail to keep those women from killing his sorry ass.)

The Spud Stud has no set breeding season—he is set to go, all the time, year round, day in, day out. Nothing short of death of the entire creature diminishes his drive or fails to give him an erection. Whatever the "pompitous of love" is, the Spud Stud is *it*. And, of course, a true Spud Stud can only be really, truly happy with the Shazzam Yam, the ultimate Queen of the Universe. No need to describe this one—you all know who you are.

# 2

## Stocking the Stable

Once you are officially out there in the real world, meeting people becomes problematic. I say meeting "people" instead of meeting "men" because it seems to be a big deal for everybody, not just us. We can't find them and they can't find us and that's just a mystery because it seems like if we're all out hunting for each other, we'd just run into each other sooner or later, wouldn't you think? Of course, the ideal thing would be if we could just stay in school forever: Everybody's all hemmed up in there in a contained area where they are easy to find. Plus, nobody's got much of a job or anything pressing that they've got to be *doing* on a regular basis, so you have a lot more time to devote to scoping each other out and fooling around.

My friend Joyce Scherer wrote and asked me a bunch of questions regarding romance and men and women and mistakes they might make in the Romance Department. First of all, I needed to give her a definition of the word *romance*, since I could see already wherein the problem lay. Romance is a widespread, regularly occurring illusion/delusion that strikes females almost exclusively and causes them to imagine that males can be somehow transmogrified into something Other Than Men— in spite of the fact that everybody knows you can't make nothing but a man out of 'em. There is no data on how "romance" manifests in men because there are no documented cases on file.

The mistake that women make in the Romance Department is that they continue to look for men there. Men are not *in* the Romance Department; they are in the Beer and Power Tools Departments. Those other people you see wandering around in the Romance Department? Those are other *women*. Men do not make mistakes in the Romance Department because they do not go *into* the Romance Department. To do that, they would first have to acknowledge the existence of the Romance Department, and they don't.

Joyce wanted to know if food figured into the Queenly Romance Department, and I said absolutely, yes. Food plays a vital role in the Romance Department because it gives us (women) something to entertain ourselves with when we discover that there are no men in there.

# Stocking the Stable

Joyce had the idea that maybe men's idea of romance was for us to show up naked with the remote control, but I pointed out two major flaws in her theory. The first, of course, is that she left beer out of the equation. The second is that if the remote control is even in the room, there's no point at all in us being naked, unless we're just hot or something, on account of he will not notice us at all.

Finally, Joyce wanted to know if age changes romance—guess she figures I'm old enough to know this by now. I told her no, age doesn't change romance at all. Women are still looking for it, and men are still in the Beer and Power Tools Departments. Nothing *ever* changes—it only gets more the same. However, I have personally discovered that there is Large Fun to be had by venturing into the Beer and Power Tools Departments!

As long as you're headed to Power Tools, let me just say two words: Home Depot. (Queen Marsha says that on her particular home turf, Lowe's attracts a higher-quality clientele, and I postulate that this will vary from region to region, so you'll need to make exploratory trips for research in your own locale.) This would be the watering hole for one of the Five Men You Must Have in Your Life at all times (one to talk to, one to dance with, one who can pay for things, one to have great sex with, and *one who can fix things*). Home Depot is mecca, nirvana, heaven—it is their happy place. (The Cutest Boy in the World and all his construction-type buddies call Home Depot "church." It's where they worship and give thanks.) It's like if you go to a shoe sale: All the women are happy, right? Same thing in Home Depot: The guys are all in an altered state, total bliss registering on their earnest little faces. All you have to do is cruise the aisles until you find one you like and then ask him a question. You know how they just purely love for us to ask 'em questions about how to *do* stuff. What they really, *really* love is for you to ask *them* to do it *for* you and then to sit there and watch them do it and ooh and aah over the performance. Don't do that unless you really want 'em, though; you can hardly drive 'em away with a stick after that.

Bookstores are also good places to find guys—you definitely want one who can *read*. And in a bookstore you can spy on him and see not only what he's reading but *how*. If he moves his lips when he reads and/or traces the words with his finger, you might want to move him to the B list. I will recall for y'all that I met the Cutest Boy in the World at a Barnes & Noble in Mobile, with subsequent encounters at the Page and Palette Bookstore and Over the Transom Bookstore, both in Fairhope, Alabama. Only after meetings in the sacred confines of those hallowed havens of literature, smack up to their very high brows in culture and intellectually stimulating stuff—only *then* did I arrange to meet up with him at the Flora-Bama Lounge (arguably the best beach bar/dive in the entire continental U.S. of A.). Another thing about bookstores: They are generally pretty well lit and everybody is pretty much sober in 'em—including you. Assuming you're sober as you're reading this, we shouldn't have to say any more about that.

## Stocking the Stable

Class reunions after number twenty-five or so are veritable hotbeds of, well, hot beds. Everybody is kinda over themselves by this point. You're no longer "fixing to" do anything; you're pretty much doing it or happy to admit that you're just not gonna do it ever and it's okay. There's not much mystery about how you'll turn out. You've already turned out about as much as you're going to. A lot of folks have grown kids by then and they're ready to focus a little more on themselves again. And then there you are, all cute and darling, and how in this world did he ever let you get away, and what a bonanza—you are also available at the moment. This is his lucky day and perhaps yours as well. There is no love like an old love. They will always see you through young eyes, which is a blessing in itself, but the other really good thing is they also see you through *old* eyes— as in eyes that are *very* old and therefore maybe not functioning so hot anymore, get it? Cataracts are wonderful things, but with macular degeneration—now, there you go—you will be positively stunning! The only thing better is the absolute dark, but it's just not constant enough, y'know? Deteriorating eyesight is definitely the way to go. It must be said that our own vision is perhaps not quite so keen anymore, either—just in case he also has some, shall we say, figure flaws that will require overlooking.

And let's hope that he does have a physical imperfection or two. I mean, I cannot imagine anything worse than hooking up with some Chippendale-looking specimen in my current (and ongoing) condition. Just as an old guy will always think I am young and cute, a big ole bubba with a beer gut will make me look positively elfin in comparison.

One of the Queens, Tammy, and I had a wonderful visit with our friend Wandelle, who moved off to Houston right after college and we hardly ever get to see her anymore. As soon as we covered how great we all looked, how cute our respective shoes were, the quality of Wandelle's tan and Tammy's total lack thereof, plus the condition of our various mamas, the conversation came around to men—namely, who's got one and what's wrong with him today. Wandelle, we could tell, was holding out on us somehow. We sensed, in that way that women do, that we weren't getting the full details of her current relationship, details to which we were entitled. She left us no choice but to double-team harangue her until she caved and gave it up. The tidbit she finally reluctantly shared with us was the twenty-year difference in their ages. Judging from our own experiences, we naturally assumed that she was dating a thirty-year-old. Imagine our shock and utter envy when she revealed that, no, he was seventy and some change—but, she hastened to assure us, he was an extremely active seventy-plus-change and very vigorous in every way.

We were struck dumb by the mere thought of how our lives would be transformed by dating the Old. I've long been a proponent of this concept on account of the opportunity it affords us to be young and cute forever. Our friend Wandelle is a case in point. *Wandelle* was not interviewing plastic surgeons and saving up for a face-lift. *Wandelle* was not the least bit worried about putting on a few pounds. Grandpa likes her a little pudgy 'cause it helps keep his old ass warm at night. She just flat out said to our faces, "I am not afraid to eat." We would kill for that to be our mantra. But who am I kidding? That *is* our mantra.

One of our Kentucky Queens, Benita, wrote me a year or so ago that she was just about to hit the dating trail again. She was post-divorce after spending ten years hauling two kids into semi-adulthood and getting her law firm up and going, and she was just about to have a date with a man she hadn't seen since they were seventeen. She was, in a word, petrified. Fortunately for all concerned, she chose that particular time to read *The Sweet Potato Queens' Book of Love*. She said it gave her the nerve to find herself—the woman pushed so far back inside her, it was questionable whether or not she still existed. She was thinking about seeing this long-lost guy and she wanted to know what I thought about it. Well, y'all know without reading further what I advised her to do! I told her to get on out there and see about her life and have some *fun*. See what happens with that man! Well, to make a long and lovely story short and sweet, she reports, they dated for a year and then he (Jack) proposed and then she said yes and then they went to Jamaica to practice up for the honeymoon—always a good plan! When she saw his eighty-two-year-old mother for the first time in thirty years, our Benita was at a Halloween party, dressed as—what else?—a Sweet Potato Queen. I just teared up reading it, I swear. I'm so proud.

Precious Pam, BJ director and spiritual adviser of the Chili Pepper Queens and proud leg-knife owner, wrote that she met the cutest guy she'd ever seen in five o'clock Friday-afternoon traffic on I-285, that horrid freeway circling Atlanta. Since the traffic barely moves on this particular roadway, they had a fair amount of time for eyeballing and grinning at each other from their respective vehicles. Pam got a tad nervous when her exit came up, and danged if it wasn't his, too. Even more unnerving was when recognition struck that he not only took the same exit, he lived in her very own apartment complex! A few days later, they spotted each other again at a volleyball game on the premises and they acknowledged each other politely, if some- what warily. That night he and his buddy knocked on her door, declaring themselves to be the Official Welcoming Committee. They wanted to welcome her to the neighborhood and offered up kisses, which seems pretty neighborly to me. Apparently she felt pretty welcome. That was sixteen years ago and she's been married to her highway man ever since.

Funerals are excellent meeting grounds as well. Unless the recently departed is one of your own personal nearest and dear- est, then you're not likely to be so broken up as to be impervi- ous to the charms of the other attendees. An added benefit is the ready-made conversation-starter the occasion, tragic though it may be, provides. You can compare notes on how you came to be acquainted with the deceased; you can discuss the appear- ance of the corpse, the cause of death, and the responsible par- ties, if any. Plenty of other people around are themselves likely to be good talking points—those with unfortunate orthodontia and facial tics, not to mention truly terrible hair and wardrobe selections, and there's always the titillating possibility of bad behavior on the part of assorted family members, in-laws, and neighbors, especially at the home visitation.

My sister, Judy, and I were fortunate enough to be in attendance at a post-funeral feed once where the bereaved's next-door neighbor's mother, Maylene, who didn't know the deceased or any of the survivors, was in town from L.A. (that would be Lower Alabama) for a monthlong visit. Maylene didn't intend to be left out of any goings-on, and so she just tagged right along to the funeral. She sure wasn't gonna miss out on the eats, so she came traipsing across the yard wagging a container of *store-bought* Jell-O salad, if you please, and just waded right on in amongst the funeral party. As luck would have it, she found the folks on the back porch with the hooch. This is how you know in the South that the grieving family is Baptist: There's a small crowd out on the back porch commiserating with Jim Beam and everybody knows it, but everybody participates in the charade that it's not happening because, of course, nobody in *this* house drinks! Of course not.

Maylene had sized up the joint the second she hit the door and saw everybody drinking sweet tea and grocery store–brand diet drinks, and she fast-tracked it to the back porch, pausing only long enough to hand off the Jell-O salad to the church lady in charge of receiving and recording food offerings and to grab a couple deviled eggs, a pimento cheese sandwich, and a Styrofoam cup. Then Maylene wedged on out the back door, cozied up to the old boy with the bottle, and held out her empty vessel, allowing as how she didn't mind if she did. In under an hour, the first bottle had been drained and its successor was dwindling. The noise from the back porch was beginning to filter into the living room—well, actually it was beginning to drown out conversations on the entire block. Judy and I worked our way through the house to a vantage point by a window where we could view the back porch drama as it evolved—or devolved, depending on how closely related you might be to the participants. Since me and Judy had no dog in this hunt whatsoever, we were enjoying it all hugely.

At one point we could tell that something important had gone missing. Through the window, we could see Maylene crawling about the porch on her hands and knees, listing first to one side almost to the point of falling over before overcorrecting her four-point stance, then listing to the other side. We could also see that her polyester slacks and tunic top were both major players in what appeared to be a wedgie of potentially life-threatening proportions. When her lumberings brought her face around in our direction, we became instantly aware of that for which she was searching so intently—her teeth. Decorum demanded that we make a speedy retreat from the premises.

Now, the ideal situation here would be that, as you are standing by the window, peering out at Maylene getting shit-faced and losing her false teeth in the bargain, a likely-looking fellow would sidle up, join you, and even contribute some snappy commentary to the whole affair. His sense of humor alone would be enough to grant him Serious Consideration Status. Also there would be probably fifteen or twenty people right there in the room with you who know him and can offer personal testimony to his level of worthiness. Good advance info can be invaluable, as you well know.

Here's something worthy of your consideration: firemen and/or paramedics! (Will we ever recover from that fireman episode on *Sex and the City?* Every time it's going to be rerun, somebody posts it on our message board so we don't miss it. It's nearly enough to drive one to arsonize one's own home, I swear.) Queen Ellen wrote me with the stellar recommendation of these helpful types. She so rightly pointed out that they are on twenty-four-hour shifts, so when they're off work, they're available to cut the grass, run the errands, and whatnot while you're at work. Then they're around to play with for a couple nights as well before they go back to work. And when they aren't with you, you know exactly where they are—all night long. They're either working or sleeping in their own beds, alone, since they got no sleep a-tall on that awful twenty-four-hour shift. (I think I smell smoke just thinking about 'em.) Ellen said that her personal beloved consort is a paramedic—"which requires a body to kill for and a kind and gentle heart." Mmm-hmm—and just a 911 away!

My very favorite Texas Queen told me that she was dancing on a table when she met this one guy. She had gone to an out-of-town bar with her married girlfriend for a little "out of pocket" experience. This was hardly the first and it most certainly was not the last time Miss Plano was dancing above the floor, but on this one particular occasion, she was just minding her own business, dancing on a table in a honky-tonk, when this cute guy jumped up on there with her and asked if she wanted to dance with him. "Why not?" seemed to be the words of the hour, and so he did. Later, the two of them went for coffee with her girl-friend—who was still married but apparently absentminded about it—and a gentleman of recent acquaintance. After a short time, those two went AWOL and our Queen found herself fairly stranded in a coffee shop with a fancy-dancing cowboy. Huh—now what? she wondered. She wasn't about to go back home without her friend and try to sidestep the husband in residence, so the boot-scooter invited her home with him to wait it out. When they got in his car, he insisted she fasten her seat belt, so she felt safe with him. Short of the long—two years later, she married the guy she met on the table.

You know how Dear Abby or Ann Landers or one of those deals is always running those "how we met" letters? Well, I've never seen one anywhere to beat the story I got from Queen Geneva in Saltillo, Mississippi. It's just about the sweetest thing I ever heard. See if you don't just tear up reading it.

Geneva and Don had lived in Saltillo all their lives. Back in the eighties, Don was a pretty well-to-do fellow in those parts.

## Stocking the Stable

On New Year's Eve in 1989, however, he walked into a church party in Baldwyn, Mississippi, and was moved by something—we may never know what—to commence shooting off not only his mouth but also his 9-millimeter. Apparently he decided right then and there that a girlfriend needed killin'. Fortunately, he didn't succeed in carrying that out, but he did manage to get himself shot, so by and by, he found himself in the Prentiss County jail for a few months, and then they sent him off to Whitfield, the state mental hospital, for a couple weeks of evaluation, and then they sent him on up to Memphis to hang out at the Mid-South Hospital for a bit.

After Don had been in Memphis about a month, who should show up but our Geneva. It seems that Geneva had had a little "spell" and removed a telephone from its usual spot at work, and she was sent away for a little "rest." So here they are in the mental hospital, as Geneva explains, "Don for shootin' a couple people—flesh wounds only—and me for absolutely losin' my mind and rippin' the phone off the wall at the pharmacy where I was employed." Geneva, at the time, was still married to her first husband ("a mean old fart") and she wasn't "looking for no new boyfriend in the nuthouse," but she and Don just sparked to each other. By the time they were released from the hospital, Geneva had decided she was going to leave that first husband, and Don—well, Don wasn't looking real forward to going back to the Prentiss County jail, so they both took their AmEx Golds and headed to Las Vegas. (Well, what would *you* have done?) They had themselves a fine time, going to shows and rafting down the Colorado River and I don't know what all, but the upshot is this: Don ended up having to give the folks at Parchman Penitentiary about fifteen months, and sweet Geneva went to see him every other Sunday the whole entire time. When he got out, they got married a week later, and they've been happily married ever since.

It all just goes to show you, Geneva says, that there's somebody out there for everybody, even if you have to go to the mental hospital to find him. I told her that was an odd turn of events. Most of us feel like we need to go there *after* we've found 'em—but hey, whatever works, and this apparently did with utterly felicitous results, so we're tickled.

It is true that we just never know when and where love will pounce on us, and our subsequent behavior is testimony to our complete lunacy while under love's influence. Our very own Official SPQ Songstress, Kacey Jones, sings a mournful lament all about ordering pizza one dark and lonely night, only to have it delivered by a guy—a reeeally good-looking guy. How good-looking was he? Well, he was good-looking enough that she ordered pizza every single night for the next month, trying—unsuccessfully—to get the same delivery guy. And don't you imagine that pizza place knows it? He is their ringer. They prolly send that guy out on all single-woman deliveries—one time—knowing they'll get about a billion reorders from women trying to get the same guy back again. And what about all the confused subsequent delivery guys wondering how come these women get all dolled up just to stay home and order pizza? If you're thinking of ordering pizza tonight, get as cute as possible. Tonight might just be *your* night for Pizza Romeo. Being prepared is a fundamental Queenly trait.

## PART II

# Distinguishing Behavioral Traits

# 3

# Us and Them*

In case you haven't noticed—there's Us and there's Them, and sometimes it's hard to tell that the two even belong to the same species. Honestly, don't you just wonder sometimes where they come from—and why? Somebody sent me an e-mail recently bemoaning the manifold sins of her husband and her own

---

*Note to readers: If you are personally acquainted with Jeff Foxworthy, I wish you'd do us all a favor and send him this whole entire chapter. He may be the only person on earth with whom we could hope to discuss these matters and have any hope of Getting to the Truth.

apparently boundless stupidity for putting up with it all. The subject line read MARS AND VENUS, IN A FIT OF INSANITY, DECIDE TO HAVE A FAMILY.

I mean, really, if you join a sorority—not that I would ever suggest such a thing, but just suppose you do—what happens? You go to teas and parties and you and your big sister buy each other silly gifts, silly songs are sung, even sillier games are played—it's all mild-mannered and sickly sweet. I cannot recall ever hearing of anyone dying of alcohol poisoning at a sorority initiation because the big sisters held the pledges down and poured whiskey down their throats, have you? Girls do not, generally speaking, hit each other repeatedly with paddles, do they? Would a Chi O ever bypass the clasp mechanism on a pledge pin and simply plunge the sharp point directly into the soft and unsuspecting breast of the pledge? No. Nor would a Tri Delt. It simply is not done. If you want any of these things or if you'd like to be forced to have sex with a farm animal (we assume it's not exactly consensual for the animal, either)—if you want that kind of thing, you'll just have to go somewhere else, namely a fraternity house, and you're gonna need to be a *guy* as well.

Certainly not the least of the differences between Us and Them would be their utter fascination and total preoccupation with our anatomy. My good friend Smokey Davis from Mobile, Alabama, once shared this illuminating tidbit of Man Lore: "Y'know," Smoke said, "the problem is, once you've seen one pussy, you just wanna see 'em *all.*" Huh. Well, time and the generations do seem to bear that out! I suppose it's not altogether a bad thing, since, last time I checked, we females do own all of them, and I reckon if there's an edge to be had in the universe, that could be ours.

Back in 1977, when I went to work for the YMCA in Jackson, Mississippi, they were opening a brand-new facility and the national organization had recently made a policy change to eliminate discrimination in memberships, meaning that even women could now join. A large percentage of the heretofore all-male membership did not exactly rejoice over this policy change, since they had been going there for the specific purpose of *avoiding* women—wives, girlfriends, secretaries—all of whom were constant sources of demand on supplies of time and money, energy and effort.

Imagine my surprise, upon entering this bastion of guyness for the first time, when I walked upstairs to the indoor running track, which was elevated above the floor in the beautiful new gymnasium, and there on the walls were spanking new signs bearing the legend PLEASE DON'T SPIT ON THE WALLS. I was mystified. "We need a *sign* for this?" I queried. Should I infer from this notice that in areas where there was no sign that wall-spitting was implicitly encouraged? If there were no signs on these walls, would other people come in and experience a triumphant thrill? "Hot damn, Bubba! Git on up here! We can spit on the walls, son!" Not only were there multiple signs telling us where we should not/could not spit, but there were actual factory-made, built-in metal-basin things specifically *for* spitting, with signs above these saying EXPECTORATE HERE. If I'm lyin', I'm dyin'! I swear to you it's the truth. There were and are these spit basins right next to almost all the water fountains, and when you turn on the water fountain, the spigot in the spittoon turns on at the same time to wash away any spit left malingering in the basin by—gasp!—surely not inconsiderate spitheads, who have neglected to "flush"? It looks disturbingly like a latrine, actually. That brings up another Guy Thing we'll speak more about later. For now, let me just say that in predominately female locales, there is not now, has never been, nor will there ever be a need for a sign that addresses the issue of spitting. We do not need to be told not to spit *anywhere*. We already know this and we do not chafe against it. It's okay with us, really. It was not part of the ill-fated Equal Rights Amendment; it has never figured even to a small degree in the women's movement. If we need to spit, we will do so, and we will do it where it belongs to be done—in private, along with a host of other acts of a personal nature that other people, namely *guys*, insist on doing not just in public but whenever possible literally in the actual *eye* of the public. Of course, there's another element at work here with this whole spitting thing, and that is the Southern Factor. Men Down Here are apparently afflicted with uncommon and unwieldy levels of phlegm, requiring them to spit and spit often. I have been literally all over this country and seen the men they've got in those Other Places, and guess what? They don't spit. You can take 'em outside and walk 'em around for hours and hours, and they won't spit once. But in downtown Jackson, Mississippi, at noontime, you can pick a spot—any spot—and sit there and watch hundreds of men go by—in business suits, no less—and more than half of them can be counted on to hock up something and deposit it on a sidewalk at least once before they get from point A to point B. Five minutes before, they were in a boardroom with dozens of people—mostly other men—and not only were none of them spitting, none of them appeared to be drowning from the urgent need to do so. But you get 'em outside, and it's spit or go blind. And that's on a city street. Lordhavemercy. Take 'em out in the country, in a field somewhere, and you have got to pick your spot wisely.

As I continued my initial tour of the shiny new YMCA facility, I encountered yet another male anomaly, this time in the men's health club. There I found a spacious massage room, with enough tables for three patrons to get a rub simultaneously. Now, that's kinda weird right there. Women wouldn't want to be in a room with other women getting a massage. We want to be in semi-darkness with soft music playing, and we want to be alone with our masseuse. For one thing, we like to keep to an absolute minimum the number of people who could see us naked. And that's yet another difference between Us and Them. Men do not care how many people see them naked, and they really don't care how repulsive the sight is to those people. We would rather pluck out the eyeballs of everyone in the room than risk being seen in the altogether. And we obsess endlessly about how repulsive that sight would be—it's our pet nightmare.

The group massage room gave me pause, but what I found next absolutely floored me—the nap room. As God is my witness, I swear to you, right next door, just a few short steps from the massage tables, was a dark, soundproof room with a bunch of cots in it, with sheets and blankets and pillows and everything. *A nap room!* A room for the express purpose of providing a dark, totally quiet, *secret* place for a bunch of guys—whose wives, girlfriends, and secretaries think they are working like dogs—to sneak off, in the middle of the damn day, and *take naps!* They have paid money to join an establishment that will provide them with not only an alibi but also a time and place to commit the crime. And this establishment has spent money to *build* them just such a place. And, believe you me, if you build it, they *will* come. I defy you to show me an organization that provides, as part of its service to its female members, a place to take a nap, and I further challenge you to find a woman who would *do* such a thing! The very idea—going out someplace in *public* to take a fucking nap!

I think of that poor benighted Betty Crocker, writing that happy homemaker crap and *daring* to suggest that if we should find our spirits and energy flagging—what with all the scrubbing and the washing and the sewing and the ironing and the cooking and the child-rearing and the whatnot—then just maybe, certainly not on a regular basis, mind you, but every once in a while, if we are really just about to fall over dead, we could maybe just stretch out for a couple of minutes on the cool linoleum of our freshly scrubbed and waxed kitchen floor. And all those years she spent slaving away with rarely so much as even a quick breather on the tile, what was *Mr.* Crocker doing? He was off at the Y, taking whirlpools, getting massages, and having full-blown, in-the-bed, in-the-dark, middle-of-the-day *naps*, and then coming home in the afternoon, expecting her to be there waiting on his sorry ass with cocktails, clean, quiet children, and a home-cooked dinner. No wonder guys are getting beaten to death with shoes.


I alluded earlier to the fact that the spit stops at the Y look suspiciously like latrines, and I promised to get back to that subject later, and so now, here we are. We were recently in a place of business where the restroom doors opened directly off the sales floor itself. There was, I swear to you, a sign on the men's room door that read GENTLEMEN—PLEASE CLOSE DOOR WHILE IN USE. Okay, the fact that there was a sign tells us that there was a *need* for a sign—predicated, no doubt, upon repeated instances of guys going in there and just whipping out and going to it, with the door standing wide-ass open and all. Wouldn't *their* mamas be proud? This had apparently happened so much that the salespeople just got fed up with having to take time away from active customers to walk over there and holler at the guys for having the manners of a he-goat and closing the door for them.

Then one time in a large warehouse, we saw, on walls, especially in the corners, signs that read NO PISSING. These were not crude, hand-lettered signs, but manufactured printed plastic ones. Again, we need a sign for this? Certainly no sign would indicate a PISS AT WILL zone. (And how about the fact that somewhere out there a sign company actually manufactures NO PISSING signs! I guess the person who makes them is grateful, on some level, that boys will be boys.)

Now, every man living has or has had a mama sometime, somewhere, and there has not been a mama in the history of the world who did not attempt to impart to her offspring information about where and where not to pee, along with other various and sundry rules about manners and consideration for others. How come it is that only the *girl* children have retained these lessons?

You do not and will not ever need a sign asking women to close the bathroom door while they use the facilities. Nor will it ever be necessary to outline for us the locations where it is/is not acceptable for us to pee. We want to pee only in an actual bathroom, with an actual (working) toilet, and certainly with an actual door. We will close it, and we will utilize any and all locking apparati available to us. The whole public-peeing thing just does not hold for us the same allure it holds for guys.

Furthermore, we do not feel compelled to "mark" places we've been by peeing on them. (Genteel Southern ladies prefer to say "tee-tee" or "wee-wee," but neither one seems appropriate in this context.) The very first thing the Cutest Boy in the World does upon arrival at his mama and daddy's house on the side of the mountain beside Lake Ouachita in Arkansas is run to the back deck and pee off of it into the treetops. I have yet to succumb to this urge. Actually, I've yet to experience that urge in the slightest. I don't ever feel even a twinge of desire to run out there and hang my ass over the side of the railing and urinate. How can this be? How can something be utterly irresistible to one person and hold not a smidgen of appeal for another?

I have actual photographs of the Cutest Boy in the World, spanning his entire lifetime, peeing with pride in exotic locations. To name a few: one of him peeing off the very edge of Victoria Falls and looking smug about his personal contribution to the swirling torrents; another, off the summit of Mount Kilimanjaro (it's worthy of note and salutation that he could even find the little fella, since it was *twenty below* up there); and one that's titled on the back "The Source of the Nile." There are photos of him peeing off the backs of moving boats in the middle of the Gulf, and off the tops of tall buildings, and out of trees—forty-one years' worth of photographs of the man peeing everywhere in the world *but* a bathroom. In contrast, even though I have a ten-year jump on him in life experience, not one single photograph, of which I am aware, depicts me in that endeavor. And oddly enough, I do not feel slighted by this omission.

# 4

## Man Ears and Other Guy Stuff

O kay, now here's something true about men: No compliment is too outrageous for a man to believe. It does not matter what the truth is or how far away from anything like the truth what you say to him is. If you say something favorable to him about himself, you can rest assured that he will believe it. He will believe it with all his heart and mind and soul. You don't even have to pretend to be sincere about it. He can be standing there, beer gut hanging to his knees and most of its hairy mass protruding way out from under a too-small T-shirt that says A LITTLE POONTANG NEVER HURT ANYBODY, camouflage pants held up with hunter-orange suspenders, and a hat with fake turds on it. And you can look at him with dead eyes and say, "Oh. Nice outfit," and he will just wag all over like a big ole dog. Men have no shame. None. The gene is missing from the entire pool. And you can go to just about any swimming pool or beach anywhere any hot summer day and see proof positive.

My friend Robin used to get married as a hobby—until her dream boy, Paul, came along and put a stop to it. Now she's just married to him all the time and she likes it. Anyway, this one ole boy she married one time liked to think he could cook, and she loved him enough at the time to allow him to continue, unabashedly, in that delusion for quite some time. And so it came to pass that one Fourth of July they were having a big party. Her friends made up the majority of the guest list, but he scraped up a few coworkers of his own to invite, and so, of course, he wanted to show off his cooking skills for them by preparing a brisket. Well, first he smoked the thing. Since using a smoker was one of the many culinary skills that eluded him, it came out like a large rubber boot. Then, with no marinade or preamble of any kind, he simply threw the thing on the grill and proceeded to cook that huge slab of rubberized red meat for about four hours until it was not only rubber, it was black rubber as well. Robin said he could not have been prouder of a thirteen-inch dick.

Fortunately, shortly after removing the burnt boot from the grill and displaying it proudly on a serving platter, some urgent matter required his attention in the kitchen (thanks in no small part to one of Robin's friends/coconspirators). This left the brisket unattended, and Robin seized not only the opportunity but the brisket itself, and with nary a moment's hesitation, she flung the offending meat up on the roof, where it landed with a decided *whump* that did little to cause the observers (Robin's friends, all) to feel they had been deprived.

By and by, the Ghastly Gourmet reappeared on the patio and observed the totally empty brisket platter. Robin and all her buddies stood there with scarcely a smirk on a single face, declaring that it was the best thing that any of them had ever eaten and, though they were embarrassed to admit it, they had eaten the entire thing completely up amongst themselves, and wasn't it a shame nobody else was gonna get any—but damn, that thing was fine. We do not doubt for one second that he took it all as the gospel truth. I'm sure he's somewhere this very day, still believing that he is some kind of fine barbecuing fiend. (Robin dang near killed herself the next day trying to retrieve the thing from the roof. It's apparently really hard to climb a ladder when you're laughing like a loon.)

But you know, it doesn't really matter what we say to 'em, because it's not what they actually hear. This is because of the Man Ears Phenomenon. Here's how it works: If a female person says something to a male person, something about the timbre or pitch of her voice identifies it as "female" to his brain, which then somehow automatically takes that sound and rearranges it into something completely different before sending the signal to his hearing appendages, which appear on the surface to the ignorant, naked eye to be regulation ears. But no, they are, in reality, now Man Ears.

It's kind of like talking to your dog—only with less positive results. With your dog, no matter what you say, he pretty much hears "Good dog," "Pretty dog," "Smart dog," "Are you hungry?" "Wanna play?" and/or "Go lie down." And that's okay because he's a dog and your expectations don't really go much beyond that. Unless your dog is, like, Lassie or Rin Tin Tin or Benji or something, you don't really expect him to earn a living or indeed to contribute much to the household other than sweet looks and doggie love. (This is not to be confused with doggie-*style* love, which is, of course, popular with all breeds, including those that wear pants.)

But that dog-in-pants that you're involved with—you need a bit more from him, and therein lies the problem. If you expect to have any hope of getting him to do anything you want, you have to be able to communicate with him, and that means you have to figure out a way to get past the Man Ears. The Man Ears, like the Dog Ears, hear praise for every aspect of his being, but especially for his sexual prowess/expertise/equipment and his ability to fix things. Whether the adulation he hears reflects reality has no bearing whatsoever on what the Man Ears hear—or upon his subsequent offers/suggestions/pleadings for sex of every imaginable description and plenty that are practically unimaginable by most people.

For instance, if you were to say to a man something like "Let's watch TV," you think you have just suggested that you'd like to sit, or possibly recline, perhaps next to him, and certainly in the same room, and that you'd like to turn on a mutually agreeable television program and view it simultaneously with him. You envision that this will entail scarcely any brainwave activity in either of your respective skulls and no physical activity whatsoever, except possibly moving assorted foods and beverages from their containers to your own personal mouths and performing whatever physical action is necessary for you to swallow them without choking. That is pretty much the sum total of what you *think* you just suggested to the man, and you couldn't be *more wrong.* See, when you said, "Let's watch TV," those words hit his brain and he thinks, Maybe when we turn on the TV, we will have somehow picked up the porn channel, and there will be a really hot scene on there! In reality, through the magic of Man Ears, what you just said, as far as he's concerned, is "I can't wait to give you a blow job." And you know, come to think of it, if you could figure out a way to accommodate him and still see the television, you would never have to watch *Monster Garage* again. Hell, you could watch *Beaches* and *Bridges of Madison County* back to back all night long and he'd never even know it. (Mark my words: Some guy will invent something to facilitate this before the year is out.)

If you happen to mention that there's a drip in the kitchen sink, the Man Ears will hear "Hey, Toolboy, get out that big equipment of yours and come rearrange my pipes!" If he actually *is* a Man Who Can Fix Things and you succeed in getting him to turn loose of your ass long enough to repair the leak, he is expecting you to sit in rapt attention and *watch* him perform the repair. Before that happens, however, you'll need first to listen to the play-by-play of his professional assessment of the problem and the many alternative remedies that could be employed, with the attendant pros and cons of each, and the tools and supplies required. After the one true way is selected and described in minute detail, it will be necessary for you to accompany him to church (aka Home Depot) to review all of the products currently in stock (whether they have any direct bearing on the repair at hand or not) because it is forbidden to ask any employee where the needed items are located, and only pussies would actually read the signs. Even though you have gone to the store to buy a single washer the size of a dime, you will need a lumber cart to push up and down each and every aisle—because they are huge and loud and hard to steer, just like somebody else we know. Several hours and hundreds of dollars later, you will return home (scene of the original dripping sink) with all your extraneous purchases. After unloading them, it will be time for lunch, after which it will be beer and nap time, and *then*, mayhap and perchance, your sink will get fixed—but only if you sit and watch and exclaim with awe and wonder over the entire process, which should, to his way of thinking, be concluded with the ubiquitous blow job. And *that*, ladies, explains why it costs so freakin' much to get a plumber to come do the repair: If there's no blow job at the end of the deal, it costs a lot to make it worth their while to leave home.

There is virtually no sentence simple and straightforward

enough to circumvent the Man Ears. "Let's stop on the way home and get a bottle of wine" gets translated by Man Ears into "I'm dying to have sex in the Miata—actually, right here, in the liquor store parking lot." "Can you help me unzip this dress?" somehow becomes "Right here, right now, with the curtains open, to hell with the neighbors—they're just jealous!" "I've got twenty-five more bags of groceries out there, can you give me a hand?" is heard as "I'm serious—I really do want to do it right this second on the kitchen table!" Now, these are the Man Ears of a relatively happy guy—a well-adjusted, fairly self-confident one with reasonable expectations in the sexual supply-and-demand department.

If, on the other hand, he's out of whack in any area of his life, the Man Ears are even more trouble. If his job is in jeopardy, look out—the Man Ears are harbingers of death. When you say, "Your friend Dave seems nice," he hears, "That Dave—now, that's a *man*. Whoooboy, he's so much hotter than *you*." If his attempts at square-pegging the round hole aren't working and you suggest an alternative, he is likely to hear, "You are an idiot! You can't do anything right and I'm not surprised because you have tiny genitals and you don't earn enough."

There's a fine line between "treatin' 'em like shit and never givin' 'em any" (where you are really nice to 'em in every way, but not so often as to become predictable and boring) and actually treating them like shit and *never* giving them any. The former works like a charm; the latter makes everybody, including you, miserable. You should just go on and find someone you want to be nice to on occasion. I have observed that the men who get the former treatment are the ones who, good-heartedly if misguidedly, think that everything you say to them is a sexual proposition and they are just tickled to death when it actually works out for them. The ones who really don't ever get any are justifiably sour individuals, and their Man Ears interpret everything as a slam. "Honey, roll over, you're snoring again" is heard as "Will you stop breathing?!" And he's probably not far off on that interpretation. I say, if you really do not want to have sex with him ever again in this life, either figure out why not and fix it or just cut the boy loose and go find someone you do want to play with. This comes under the Life Is Too Short/Long category.

If he's commitment-phobic and you mention that your dog died and you could use some help grave-digging, "Marry me!" is what his Man Ears are likely to hear. If the com-phobe appears to be in a funk and you dare to inquire, "Is anything wrong?" the words he hears bouncing off the walls of his pointy head are "Tell me everything! Tell me now! You have no personal space or freedom! Surrender!"

Then there are the guys who have their Man Ears on backwards or inside out or upside down or something—they just can't catch a hint with a shrimp net. One of the Queens, Tammy, has this fiancé who loves to blow into town and wait on her hand and foot, which is a good thing, because it's precisely what she has in mind. He particularly enjoys washing and detailing her automobile, which is also a good thing, because she purely despises doing it although she does enjoy having it sparkling clean and shiny. He likes to take it to one of those places where you wash and wax it yourself at one spot and then vacuum and steam-clean it at another. The closest place like this is in the 'hood, right next door to a liquor store/mini-grocery/crack dealership, but that doesn't dissuade her fiancé one bit.

A regular crowd of panhandlers hangs out in the parking lot, hassling paying customers for change, but the management doesn't run them off because sooner or later they get enough money together for a pint, some Twinkies, or a rock, and then they become paying customers, too. (Very forward-thinking on the management's part.) Anyway, the fiancé is a soft touch, so he's popular with the homeys. Tammy is always concerned that he might be killed—before he gets through with her car. One day he was reassuring her and shared a conversation he'd had with his compadres that very day, which, according to his Man Ears, was about hometowns. He explained that when one young woman in the group asked him if he was from Jackson and he said no, she told him she wasn't, either. "I'm from Coochie Sprangs," she told him, as she no doubt sprawled over the hood of Tammy's car in that provocative crack-ho way. Fortunately for Tammy's fiancé, he didn't express a desire to visit there one day, but simply washed the damn car and came on home. Tammy took matters in her own hands—literally, with the Yellow Pages— and found him a car wash in a better neighborhood.

But I can't really fault the men totally in all this, although it is tempting: They're such easy targets. No, the truth is, we women do so often *say* things totally contrary to what we actually *mean*. It's no wonder Man Ears developed. Nature is trying to evolve a self-preservation device for them—to warn them that "there's another message here—pay attention. It's important—even dangerous."

Admit it. How many times has your man of the moment fallen into a trap like this: You say, "Oh, my, isn't Dan's new girlfriend *pretty?*" and he, believing that you actually think the bitch is attractive and sincerely want him to agree with you about it (and he's eager to agree with you because all he's really thinking about is getting laid by you later), stupidly exclaims, "God, yes, she's fucking *gorgeous!*" And with those words, the End of the World is set in motion.

Of course, what you *really* meant by your question was "Dan's new girlfriend is fucking gorgeous and I am a cow. I hate myself for eating that entire pie. My clothes are about to explode from the sheer stress of trying to contain all that is me. Soon buttons and shreds of fabric will fill the air, and when the dust settles, small villages will be lost in the sudden fat-slide of my nekkidness. I used to be pretty. I remember it and the memory kills me. Look at me and love me anyway."

And what you wanted in response was "*You* are absolutely gorgeous. You are *much* more beautiful than Dan's girlfriend. That woman is only average at best. I wouldn't want to be seen with her. I can't imagine what Dan sees in her." But no. And all of a sudden, the whole night has gone to shit and he has no clue why. He was just being agreeable and looking goofily ahead to what he was pretty confident was a sure thing, and now he's sitting somewhere by himself, still horny and utterly bewildered as to where he went wrong.

We know there's no compliment too outrageous for a man to believe, and that such a belief system allows him to carry on shamelessly in public, but the truth is very few, if any, compliments are too outrageous for us to believe, either—at least in private. Although your glowing praise of our many delights will not embolden us to unseemly public performances (thankfully), they will certainly dispose us most kindly toward you behind closed doors—and isn't that what you were after all along? Really, Dumbo, open up them big ears and listen to me: *We are so easy.*

# 5

# And Still More About
# "The Promise"

Man alive! (Or, if you prefer, "Holy shit!") Did we forevermore open that big old worm can when we took it upon ourselves to present in plain, clear words "The Sweet Potato Queens' Promise" and to openly discuss its merits! (Please refer to *The Sweet Potato Queens' Book of Love*, chapter 2, in which we discuss the True Magic Words, 100 percent guaranteed to get any man in the world to instantly and cheerfully do your every bidding. Hint: We promise 'em a blow job—with the emphasis on the promise, not delivery thereof. Actually, that's not a hint—it's the whole thing.) Hardly a day goes by, if indeed one ever does, that I don't get at least one e-mail from some guy—whining, of course—or some Queen, usually howling, but occasionally on the horns, if you will, of a dilemma.

My good Noo Yorker friend Rachel shared with me a missive from a certain "Tim," one of her legions of boyfriends/ fiancés. Tim had just learned, from Rachel, about the Promise. He pontificated that if women-types can extend the conditional offer of a blow job in exchange for services rendered/jewelry purchased/etc., we women should know their (guys') corresponding policy regarding loyalty and listening—to a woman. Regarding loyalty, Tim felt that it was important for a man to take the side of his woman, and he wisely noted that he implied no actual ownership of the woman in the reference. But Tim really bowed up about the listening requirement. Just because a guy is *hearing* whatever issue we're currently voicing in their vicinity, he said, we should not assume that they are understanding or, for that matter, even actually listening to us. Indeed, he said, your man can be looking at you intently with an expression of total, rapt understanding and/or sympathy/empathy, yet at this very time several ideas totally unrelated to your commentary are really occurring in his mind: (1) A huge wave of apathy regarding our problem surges through his gray matter. (2) That wave encounters another one that is anything *but* apathetic, and it has to do with wondering where the fuck the remote control is so he can turn on the game and stop even pretending to listen to us. (3) And all of *that* wave action is totally swept away by the veritable storm surge of thought that truly consumes him all his waking hours and most of his sleeping ones—and that would, of course, be "Where the hell am I gonna get a blow job?!"

Thank you, Tim! This is good information to have, although hardly what we call "breaking news." I'm sure all my readers will know instinctively how to deal with this situation in the future. For one thing, he can probably forget about ever finding that remote control.

Our precious Queen Andrea—known to her husband as "the Welcher"—wrote that she'd spent the last few years (since 1999, to be exact) on those dilemma-horns we mentioned earlier. It seems that she and her husband—along with his mother—went to a hotsy-totsy hospital fund-raiser where Wynonna Judd was performing to the utter delight of the wine-soaked crowd. We know that there was a fairly widespread case of inebriation going around on account of Wynonna had been successful in getting a bunch of tight-ass doctors up onstage with her to "dance." The doctors' efforts amounted to nervous wiggling of some of their body parts and jiggling of others (still their own), but they were inordinately pleased with themselves, naturally, in that drunk-doctor sort of way. (Actually, that state is not restricted to men in the medical profession. Come to think of it, it's not really even confined to the drunk ones.)

Anyway, Andrea was all wound up to get her husband, known to many as the Life of Any Party, up there on the stage to dazzle the crowd in his own inimitable way. And Sonny-boy's own mama was steady chiming in her support for this deal. Well, he gets Andrea off to the side and demands to know, "What's in it for *me?*" In the heat of a fairly sotted moment Andrea made a foolhardy pact with her devil. She made her husband the Promise. I guess we'd have to say she made him the Double-Secret, Triple-Platinum Promise of a Lifetime: She did, in fact, promise to give the man a blow job every night for the rest of their married lives! Now, this right here would be what they're talking about when they say an "offer he couldn't refuse."

Quicker 'n' shit through a goose, Sonny-boy hopped his happy-ass up on that stage and showed Wynonna (and the rest of the party people) what a "dancing fool" looks like up close and in person. His mama (who was unaware of the bargain struck between the couple) and Andrea were both drowning in their own mascara-stained tears and laughing like howler monkeys. All of a sudden, Wynonna says to Sonny-boy, "E-e-e-e-e-e! You're afraid of me!" But Sonny-boy doesn't miss a beat. He says right back to her, "Nuh-uh, I'm not neither, my wife's a natural redhead!" And so on and so forth. Obviously, all who were still conscious for it had a reeeeally good time. Everything went pretty well until . . . oh yeah, the fool wanted to *collect* on that Promise. Now. In fact, he has been hounding her nearly to death for the last five years about it. Now, Andrea was freely admitting to totally reneging on her Promise. Her position was that she had obviously been in an altered state when she made it and therefore incapable of entering into a binding contract and he ought to have known better then and he should certainly know better *now* and leave her alone. She had already tried, with success, the Last Resort suggested in *God Save the Sweet Potato Queens*—that being Show Up Naked with Beer. She was really worn out with that and she needed my help in negotiating something different. Andrea's best friend, Gina, had sagely remarked, "Anything you promise your husband is stupid." And if those are not words to live by, I just never heard any, so my first advice to Andrea was to hang on to Gina at all costs.

I agreed that the contract was rendered null and void by her condition at the time it was issued, but I did suggest that she proffer a compromise to effectively jerk him back in line. This would involve actually *delivering* a few times in order to lull him into the desirable pliable state. I also pointed out to her that even in her stupor, she had had the presence of mind to include a loophole in what was otherwise a very bad contract. Since she had promised him a blow job every single night of their *married* lives, she could threaten to change that state if he persisted on this course. And what do you think the judge would do when he heard that this guy had been stupid enough, first, to believe and then to try to collect on such a Promise from his lawfully wedded wife? He would, of course, grant her a speedy divorce on the grounds of Unbelievable Idiot and promptly give her all his assets, current and future. (I recommend that this argument be used only in place of an actual death threat, since many would consider even the suggestion of such utter financial annihilation to be considered cruel and unusual punishment.

Indeed, to a large percentage of the population, death would be infinitely preferable.)

Andrea might want to consider Queen Jennifer's solution. Whenever Jennifer makes the Promise to her husband, she has found it most effective to promise to give him *five* blow jobs—at some undetermined time in the future, when he is, shall we say, *up* for it. She has now made that Promise so many times that the both of them know the account can never be paid in full, and so she has made an executive decision: She is filing for chapter 11 bankruptcy on those silly Promises (certainly not her credit cards). That way she can start all over with a clean slate. This seems like a sound decision to me. After all, the bankruptcy laws were created to help those who, through no fault of their own, end up with an unmanageable load of debt. Andrea will have to be more frugal with her Promises in the future, however, since she won't be eligible to file again for seven years. With that in mind, I suggested she rein herself in on that five-at-a-time business.

But then I offered her and Andrea what I consider to be the Ultimate Weapon of Mass Destruction Against Persons of the Man-Kind: Give him what he wants till he don't want it no mo'. As my daddy would say after eating mountains of food and being offered still *more*, "Well, no, thankee, I reckon it's done got down where it ain't any good!"

I was fairly inspired when I received an e-mail from a precious little Larva Queen who said that she and her shiny new husband had gone to the beach on their honeymoon and promptly encountered a major schism in their new relationship. He wanted to have sex in the *daytime*—hel-lo!—at the *beach*— as in *when the sun is out*—and she, having good beach sense, wanted to forgo their carnal delights until after the tanning rays had dissipated. I completely understood and totally sympathized with her. The very idea! Well, he actually called *her mother* and complained (whined) about the situation. *Can you imagine?* But Mama was clearly a Queen and asked to speak to her baby girl pronto, and she delivered what was easily one of the best lines ever uttered: "Hunny, what that boy needs is a good pussy-whippin'." She so wisely advised her precious daughter—it really makes me tear up to think about it—to hang up that phone and commence to lovin' up on that boy and to continue lovin' up on him *waaay* past when he got enough. "Keep at him until he begs you to stop and then keep on until you make him cry at least once. Make it painfully clear to him that he has woefully overestimated his own personal Bite/Chew Ratio." Dutiful Daughter did as Mama said, and the happy result was that hubby got happy with nighttime nooky, and Baby Girl got a great tan. Oh, yeah, Mama is the One Who Knows Best.

# 6

## T.G.S.

T.G.S. That would be Typical Guy Shit, as in who *else* would do this? And boy hidee, they start young, too. A visit to the message board at www.sweetpotatoqueens.com one afternoon brought me to a story by one of our dear Queens, LasagnaLover. The title of the thread caught my eye: "The Taco Bell Accident." It seems that LasagnaLover was visiting a very fine Taco Bell establishment with her two little chil'ren—a baby girl, only several months old and yet already behaving with the utmost decorum in her little car seat, and a little boy, only a few years old, but already a complete and utter *boy*, as you will see.

# T.G.S.

L.L. was happily chowin' down on a taco when she became distracted by a suspicious non-taco-like scent wafting about her personal table space. She quickly checked the baby's diaper but came up empty, so she turned her gaze upon the boy, who gazed back with that look of guileless innocence they are apparently born with, because it has nothing to do with their actual state of being. She asked the boy if he had perhaps had a small accident, to which he replied in the negative. By and by, the aura thickened once more, and once more she fixated upon the boy as the obvious odiferous offender, but still he vowed there was nothing untoward in his little-boy briefs. Upon the third occurrence of the wafting odor, she was now certain the boy was guilty of soilage, and frankly, she was out of patience with his persistent denials, and she indicated all this to him in the strongest terms. The boy apparently lost patience with *her* badgering and simply hopped down from the booth, dropped trou, bent over, spread his little cheeks, and shouted, "See, Mom! It's just farts!" And that pretty well settled that.

I feel fairly comfortable in guessing that L.L. will never doubt his veracity again—at least not in public. And yes, everybody in the *en-tire* restaurant did witness the whole thing, and there was much guffawing and probably pretty serious pants-wetting in Taco Bell that day.

This next T.G.S. comes from the somewhat-older-boy faction: *Parade* magazine featured a piece about junior high schools all across the country, with interviews of students about their future aspirations, if any, as well as issues of the day that were important to them. (This reminded me of a local afternoon kids'

show, when the host asked the little beesters what they wanted
to be when they grew up. One said, "An Indian," and another one
said, "A fire truck.") The junior-high kids all sounded very grown-
up and together, and they gave some thoughtful and insightful
answers—it was quite impressive. Then I got to this one kid
from somewhere in Mississippi, who was quoted as saying something like this: "My school is really great, except the principal is
a total goober-nugget." The kid's entire name, school, town, and
state followed this pithy comment—there was no mistaking
who said it. Do you reckon he ever finished junior high? And
what, pray tell, *is* a goober-nugget? I confess, this bit of boy talk
has become one of my own personal favorite epithets, but I have
no earthly idea what it could mean. I guess you have to be a boy.

Okay, now from the even *older*-boy faction: Guy goes to a
convention out of town, bad weather causes his return flight to
be canceled, and he has to spend another night in the hotel. He
happens to meet a lovely young woman at the concierge's desk
who's in the same predicament. They strike up a conversation
and discover they're from the same town, so they agree to share
a rental car and drive home together the next morning. Guy has
no more clean underwear. He washes all of it out in the sink but,
of course, doesn't know the trick of rolling wet laundry in a
towel to speed-dry it, and so the next morning everything is
still sopping wet. He is reluctant to just swing into the lobby,
commando-style, so he decides to dry some undies in the
microwave so thoughtfully provided in his room. He puts his
underwear in there on high and gets in the shower, but when he

gets out of the shower and opens the bathroom door on his way to the kitchenette to retrieve what he thinks will be his fluffy, dry dritties, what should engulf him but billowing black smoke. The shriek of the fire alarm follows and then the cold water of the overhead sprinkler system. He clutches his towel about him and evacuates his room at the bellowed request of the firemen in the hall, which is also full of smoke. He stands shivering on the sidewalk in the early-morning light with all his fellow evacuees until the firemen give the all-clear and the guests are allowed to return to their rooms. Dressing feverishly, he slinks downstairs, sans underpants, to meet his ride, and of course, all anybody in the lobby can talk about is the fire and how it was caused by some bonehead trying to dry his underwear in the microwave. He quietly rides all the way home with his legs crossed, but there was probably no need.

One of my very favorite men in the entire world, living or dead, is a little on the shy side sometimes, and he'd shit sideways if he thought I talked about him in any of my books, so we'll just call him Joe. When Joe was in boot camp at Parris Island, he and a bunch of his buddies got liquored up—big surprise—and went en masse in search of a tattoo parlor so they could all get tattoos. They found one, of course, and they all piled in there and started the laborious process of choosing their tattoos. I imagine this would be an exhaustive ordeal. I mean, I can honestly say that I have never even owned a *dress* that I would want to wear every single day for a week, much less the rest of my life. Choosing something as permanent as a tattoo seems at best pretty much out of the question. How many things that you thought were just so cute ten years ago still hold that same appeal for you today? For me, two words would be enough to nip this whole line of thinking in the early bud stages: Herman's Hermits. Apparently other folks are more committed to their icons than I've been thus far in my life, and choosing a tattoo is something they can easily do in under an hour.

So anyway, the buddies of Joe all quickly chose a design and fell into line to get inked. Joe had his heart set on a "devil dog." (This is apparently some kind of juju for Marines, but to me it sounds like something made by Little Debbie.) He searched through all the design books, but he could not find the devil dog. Due to the fact that the group had contrived to continue drinking while in the tattoo parlor, by the time our dear Joe's time came, he was dead-ass drunk and crying. And the tattoo man said unequivocally that he had tattooed Marines who were drunk, passed out, and even *dead*, but he'd be damned if he would tattoo one who was crying. And that is how it came to pass that Joe does *not* have a tattoo of a devil dog, Little Debbie, or anything else—and his lovely bride, the diminutive Brenda Avery, is *thrilled*.

# 7

## Otherwise He's Fine

O*therwise.* Now, there's a word to put the "ick" on your "wow," if ever there was one. A few other words—*interesting*, for instance—have a similar sickening effect on us. Even years after her divorce from the Antichrist, "interesting" can send Tammy into a full-fledged attack of Distress in the Lower Tract (only readers of a certain age will recall that riveting commercial). During the course of their less-than-blissful union, Beelzebub would call Tammy numerous times throughout the day to verbally push her out of the plane at forty thousand feet with a cheery smile, best wishes, and a faulty umbrella. He usually gave several reports of how he'd been "done wrong" by his clients or his fellow employees and/or employer du jour. And then would come offhand references to wildly expensive automobile-related charges he had incurred. (Perhaps he had some bizarre version of Munchausen's by proxy—you know, that's where people get off by making other people sick and then taking them to the doctor. This guy had that, only with his *car.*)

Occasionally, the couple would actually ride in the car together, but not often: Her heart really couldn't take it. Her hands have still not completely lost their clawlike bent from her white-knuckled rides with the Devil on Wheels. But sometimes it was unavoidable and she was forced to be his passenger, and they'd be riding along when suddenly he would turn off the radio, shushing her and directing her, in a tone dripping with dread and doom, to "listen!" She would dutifully listen, although all she ever heard was her own heart thudding and the soft rustle of credit-card bills making mountains all around her. He would cock his head to one side and focus all his energies on hearing what in his mind was potentially the death knell of his beloved automobile. The man could hear sounds in that engine that no one else on earth ever heard—most especially his mechanic. This did not, however, deter said mechanic from doing what amounted to Exploratory Pocket Surgery (Tammy's pockets, naturally) and replacing many parts, both real and imaginary. It may interest you to know that the imaginary ones are even more expensive than the real ones: Imaginary repair work is much more difficult to complete, and the charges certainly reflect that.

Sometimes when Satan called her, Tammy could detect from the tone of his voice that he had wandered off from his workplace and was in a very expensive men's clothing store. She could tell this because he was nice to her, and he was nice to her because *she* had just unwittingly bought him a little something fine, say, for example, numerous pairs of cashmere socks. These are an absolute wardrobe essential here in Mississippi, where we live, because—you may be unaware of this—the temperature in the winter often plunges below seventy degrees.

Then there were the bad days. Ha-ha! You thought *those* were the bad days? Again I say ha-ha! No, those were the *regular* days. On the *bad* days, he would call and pretend to chitchat idly. Tammy still fights the automatic-gag reflex whenever someone tries to engage her in chitchat of the idle variety, on account of whenever Satan would benignly ask, "How is your day?" and she would answer, her very fine Southern upbringing demanded that she in turn ask him how *his* day was. And absolutely 100 percent of the time, he would reply with one word, and that one word was "interesting," and she would nearly vomit on the spot. "Interesting" coming from most people might introduce "I learned to solve a Rubik's Cube in under eight seconds" or "I saw the most incredible rainbow today" or "An orgasm for a pig lasts for hours." On the lips of the Hound from Hell, it invariably meant something along the lines of "I'm running from the law on account of I punched out some people at work when they fired me, and I got a ticket for double-parking [outside the wildly expensive men's store] when I went in to pick up my new Versace suit, and goddammit, wouldn't you know it, they didn't have it ready!" She finally succeeded in running him off. *Otherwise* she would have been shopping for a chipper-shredder before too long and giving him the most *interesting* day of his life. And so it was that the *otherwise* innocuous word *interesting* came to hold dire portents for our Tammy. And that brings us back to *otherwise.*

Consider the plight of Queen June, who wrote to say that, post-divorce, she had some really bad experiences with set-up dates. But there was this one particular boy—and she called him that because he was only twenty-eight, and at that, somewhat younger than she was—who she decided was worth at least a few trial runs. He was, after all, from a good family (she even indicated that he was from "cotillion stock" and seemed pleased with that), and, more important, at least to me, he was tall, dark, and smart. "Artsy" was included in the description, which usually suggests "poor," but she sensed he had "potential." So anyway, June-bug went out with Mr. Artsy Potential a couple times and she was thinking he might, in fact, turn out to be worthy, and with trashy thoughts swirling in her mind, she invited him back to her place. Of course, this is *so* the tip-off that she had Intentions.

(One of our rascally Wannabes—who must remain nameless—is forever calling me to report on the "unexpected turn of events" that seems to occur with alarming regularity on her dates. "Somehow, I have no idea how, I ended up giving him a blow job!" she confesses, and she says it in the same tone she would use if she were telling me she fell down the stairs—as if she's completely surprised by the whole thing. How it happened is beyond her. All she knows is she "started off giving him a back rub, and the next thing I knew, I was giving him a blow job!" I have heard this tale of faux-wonder so many times now, I finally asked her how come *she* is so surprised by it. I see it unfolding from the moment the words *back rub* leave her lips. As far as this little missy is concerned, "back rub" and "blow job" are definitely chronological and actually pretty much synonymous. If he can get her to rub his back, he's pretty much good to go for the full-meal deal, so to speak. But she continues to cop the coy attitude about it when she tells on herself. I guess it's a form of ReVirgination—it doesn't count if you can convince just one other person that you didn't plan it.)

But anyway, June was more forthright in her accounting of herself. She said right out front that she took Mr. Artsy Potential home in order to make the final decision on whether or not they had "dessert," and they were kinda cozy on the couch when he suddenly announced, "It's time." She was admittedly puzzled and thought he was proclaiming his leave-taking, but he simply said again, "It's time." And then he said he'd be back in a few minutes, whereupon he went into the sole bathroom in the house and holed up in there for a *very* long time. He was gone for so long, she nearly started vacuuming just to have something to do.

What June wanted to know from me was: What do the Queens think about this situation? She is of the opinion that it should be saved for marriage. Her friends were divided predictably along gender lines on the subject—the guys, who think it is such a natural, blessed event, they don't even really have to close the door all the way, and the girls, who think he should have said, "I'll be right back," and run to the gas station. Poor, they can tolerate, but never the defecating poor. This was an off-putting episode, to be sure, but *otherwise* he was fine.

I naturally wrote June a rapid response since her urgency was fairly leaping off the computer screen, and I referred her to *The Sweet Potato Queens' Big-Ass Cookbook (and Financial Planner)*, which had just hit the stands at that time, telling her that within those pages this very issue was discussed, although it was and is over the very strenuous objections of my dear editor, JoAnne, who does like to pretend that No One Does . . . you know. I told June that I understood her quandary but that I, myself, felt the problem was not so much that the boy had a healthy human bodily function to perform but rather that he chose to announce it—and in a cutesy manner at that. I really do hate cutesy in a man. I'd nearly rather that he take a dump on the floor than act cutesy about it—but that's just me. However, to my mind, it did indicate that he had an appropriate sense of embarrassment about being called by nature in such a forceful manner so early in their relationship, and therein lay the answer I offered to June: *compassion*—show some compassion. What if the roles had been reversed? What if *she* had been in *his* tiny apartment and it came upon *her* so suddenly that there was no escape since she didn't even have her own car there? June, I told her, if this is the *only* flaw in the darling boy, give your very fine sensibilities a little time to recover from this shock and see him again, keeping in mind that this may be his Pattern of Regularity, and therefore, you should linger for a good long time in the restaurant after dinner to give him time to perform it there. Or if it comes up at home again, do, by all means, get up the second he excuses himself and get busy so it's not so awkward when he returns. (At least he didn't feel "comfortable" with you. *Otherwise* he would have not the slightest qualm about farting at will and discussing properties of it.)

It's tragic how little it takes to kill a deal sometimes, isn't it? I mean, Tammy and I were on a little road trip once—when we were very young, so many years ago—and we passed some boys who were also very young and seemed to be similarly engaged in a bit of excursion diversion, and we could see plain as day that they were some of the cutest things on the road; the other cutest things on the road that day would have been *us*, naturally. They couldn't help but see how cute we were, and we couldn't help but see them seeing how cute we were, and we were pretty pleased with that, of course. But we were whizzing down the highway in separate vehicles, and so it was nothing more than a passing perk.

By and by, though, we came to a rest stop—and dang, if their car wasn't parked right out in front of the building, and dang, if the cute boys weren't all right out there in plain sight!

And we were thinking, How lucky is this? We could tell they were thinking the same thing when they saw us driving up, but they were being all cool and everything, the way boys try to be at every opportunity, and they were sauntering over to their car, which was a mostly nondescript car of the BTN variety—that would be Better Than Nothin', but not turning any heads for style. (We have some girlfriends in Yazoo City, Mississippi, who are actually older than we are, if you can imagine *that*, and as you might further imagine, the dating pool in Yazoo City, Mississippi, for women even older than we are is not exactly teeming with possibilities. The girls, therefore, have cultivated a sort of stable, if you will, of pretty much all of the available—by that they mean breathing, ambulatory, and solvent, in addition to unattached—men in their immediate vicinity for use whenever they have a need for an escort or a lightbulb changing, etc. These are the BTNs—the Better Than Nothin's, bless their hearts. They may be breathing but they don't get to breathe hard, at least not with our girlfriends—although they have been known to fib on occasion and out-and-out lie on others.)

At any rate, the cute boys were sauntering, cool-like, over to their BTN car, looking at us but pretending they weren't—very cool—until they got right up to their car, whereupon all of a sudden they started screaming like *girls* and flapping their arms in the air and running (also like girls) away as fast as their little legs could carry them. To say we were nonplussed by this odd turn of events would be putting it mildly. Our cute guys are squirrels, was the thought that immediately popped into our collective minds. Sigh.

By the time we got parked at the curb—a fair distance away from them and their BTN—they had started their reapproach to their car, and again, were making with the cool, detached saunter, and when they got almost to the car doors, the squealing, flailing, and scurrying ensued once again. Now we were laughing at them but we were still attempting to conceal that fact. We went on to the ladies', but we could tell that the mayhem was being repeated outside and we were laughing fit to kill in the stalls. When we composed ourselves and emerged, they were once again approaching the BTN, but this time on tiptoe— being very quiet and sneaky—hoping to catch the killer car napping, I suppose. I mean, we're looking at the very car that is causing them such distress and we ain't seein' nothin'. There is no visible cause for their repeated fits that *normal* people in the area can discern. And yes, everybody is pretty much laughing at them, openly by now, but the guys are so freaked out by whatever *it* is, they don't realize it.

Tammy and I were mesmerized by their act—and not a little perplexed. I mean, what was the deal, anyway? We watched for quite a little while until we just couldn't afford to give any more time to it and the novelty had started to wear off. When we were backing out of our own unhaunted parking space, we finally saw what their problem was: in a word, litter. Some asshole litterbug—and isn't *that* redundant—had blithely tossed out a scrap-filled bag from KFC and left it to ferment on the pavement in the hot Mississippi sun, and any Southerner knows what happened next. Yep, that bag of slop drew every yellow jacket in three counties. They'd piled up in that festering sack of KFC leftovers having a *feast*, and they were perfectly happy in a busy, buzzy, yellow-jackety sort of way—until these yay-hoos came and parked their big ole car on top of them. And so in typical yellow-jackety retaliation, the flying brigade would swarm about the boys in full yellow-jackety force whenever they approached their car. We were shrieking with laughter, knowing that those guys had only two choices: (1) Send one guy in as a sacrificial lamb to get stung eighty gabillion times getting in the car and moving it *off* the buggy bag so the rest of them could enter unstung, or (2) wait until sundown, when the bees would go off to nap.

We didn't have time to wait and see what the choice would be, and it was killing us. But Lady Luck was just slobbering all over us that day, and the very next time we stopped at a rest stop—Tammy has a bladder roughly the size of a smallish acorn—who should pull up as we were leaving but the Bee Boys! Apparently they either hadn't thought of the sacrificial-lamb theory or nobody would volunteer for the duty, because all of them had welts all over and they were very subdued, no doubt from the big dose of Benadryl some Good Samaritan had given them. They were not too doped up to be sheepish, however, and we just couldn't help ourselves. As we came out of the ladies', we spotted them parking their BTN, all craning their necks to make sure there was no litter in this chosen spot.

Without a word of discussion between Tammy and me, we moved of one accord. We tiptoed up—almost to their very car doors—and then broke out into hysterical squealing, beating the air and ourselves wildly, and then we ran as if demon-chased to our own car, jumped in, and sped away—amid gales of laughter that were pretty much all our own.

And so you see, an *otherwise* potential true-love match between Us and Them was foiled, spoiled, and utterly wrecked by a sack of bees.

## PART III

# Methods of Attracting Them

# 8

# I've Done a Lot More for a Lot Less

Hard to believe really, the things we'll do in the name of love. Even more head-slapping are the things we'll do for lust—or even "just to get his attention," for that matter. I claim no personal innocence in these matters—even I, your Boss Queen, have been a total igmo on more than one occasion for these very same causes. Often, the wronger a guy is for you, the more extreme your behavior will be. This is a major mystery of Womankind. Why is it we will absolutely harelip *hell* to try to get with some guy who is an absolute hound from that very place? How many times have you watched your best friend chase off after some worthless guy like a dog after a Chevy, and you know when she starts out that if and when she catches him, it will be about like Spot catching the Tahoe—heavy collateral damage for Spot, and the Tahoe won't even slow down. And how many Tahoes have you tackled in your time and barely lived to tell the tale? What *is* it that sends us tearing down the sticky, hot asphalt of love, yowling after a big-domestic-gas-guzzler-with-no-muffler-bald-tires-and-bad-upholstery kind of a guy? If I could answer that question, I don't know that I'd be rich, but I'd sure as hell be smart, 'cause nobody's answered that one since the earth cooled off enough for us to walk around on it, as far as I've heard.

Well, at least it gives us something to talk about at showers. If guys ever develop a passing interest in What Women Think and Talk About, they should spy on a wedding or baby shower—any one, it doesn't matter who it's for or who is there. The most intimate details of any experience ever survived by a woman can be heard—live and in color—at one of these female gatherings.

I'm telling you, I cannot believe that the human race is still going on. It seems to me that after the very first baby shower ever held in the history of the world, word would have gotten around, and birth, as we know it, would have been canceled due to lack of interest. From the time I was old enough to go with my mother to a shower, I have heard women telling really and truly horrific delivery room stories. Omigod, the closest thing I could liken it to is those old Tarzan movies, where the Reeeally Bad Guys chase the Good Guys down in the jungle, and then tie 'em up and haul 'em back to camp for a party. The party consisted of lots of drumming and leaping about while whooping, building to the point where they would haul out the Good Guys, one by one, for the Big Finish. Today this would be where there's a flashy fireworks display perhaps. The Big Finish for the Reeeally Bad Guys' parties was that they'd take a Good Guy and tie one of his legs to a bent-over but very sturdy sapling and the other leg to another bent-over but very sturdy sapling, and then they would let go of the saplings and *voy-ola*, the Good Guy ripped half in two, to the utter delight of the Reeeally Bad Guys. And you can only imagine the state of the remaining Good Guys waiting their turns in their respective cages, surely considered very good seats for viewing the action. This was pretty much the way I felt as a young girl regarding any potentiality for personally bearing a child one day.

I swear, to hear the women at the showers tell it, nobody ever just went in and gave birth without nearly dying or wishing they would die or wishing their husband and every other person on the planet with a penis would die. There always seemed to be a competition about who had the most intolerable level of pain, who had the biggest baby (and they were nearly always breech or worse), and, of course, who had the most cruel, heartless, and unfeeling delivery room nurses. To hear these postpartum tales led one to believe that if a woman retired as a torturer in a Turkish prison, or just got bored being one, she would hire on as a delivery room nurse. They would fiddle while Rome was yanked sideways out of your birth canal (which was always the smallest one the doctor had ever seen) and then they would stitch you up with baling wire (if you were lucky; they preferred to let you bleed to death).

I spent my entire young adult life in mortal dread of delivery room nurses. So firmly was I convinced of their treachery that when, at the age of thirty-five, I found myself in need of their services, I was . . . well, I was just in a state, is all I can tell you. I was scheduled for a C-section, and I literally got up at like three A.M. and baked about eight thousand of my famous Homade Blueberry Muffins—enough for the delivery room nurses who would actually be attending my surgery as well as all the nurses on the floor for every shift the day I arrived. I was taking *no* chances with any of them. I arrived on the scene bearing gifts—and edible ones at that. It wasn't necessary, of course: They could not have been sweeter and kinder to me. If the shower stories are true, then I'm the only woman in the history of childbearing to have a pleasant time of it. I had a blast. It was all endlessly fascinating, plus I got this really great baby out of the deal.

It doesn't hurt that I am what is known as a Good Patient. I do what the doctors say. I don't complain. I don't whine. I always thank everybody for everything they do for me, and I don't ask them to do stuff I can more easily do myself. Yes, they are paid to take care of you; they are not, however, paid to take shit from you. And they are not maids. Nurses are *people*, for crying out loud, and they are people who have a direct effect on the quality of your hospital experience; therefore, it behooves you, as the patient (read: helpless, at their mercy), to be nice to these people. I have often marveled at the sheer, stupid bravado of sick people with balls enough to treat their caregivers like crap. What are they thinking? It's the same with people who are rude to waiters and waitresses. Yes, they really will spit in your food! And they *should*. Everybody within a six-table distance of you would love to come spit in your food, you asshole—they're doing it for the team.

Moral: Be nice to people who are doing something for you, whether it's bringing drugs and bedpans or drinks and fries.

But anyway, another Favorite Topic of Women at Showers is the Dangers and Horrors of Menopause. Now, I grew up in the South, where hysterectomies came to be known as Mississippi Appendectomies. For years and years, if a woman in the South went to her gynecologist and said her period was five minutes late, early, too short, or too long—whatever—*whoosh*, out it all came! No matter what her complaint—or even if she didn't have a complaint—she had just had all the kids she was gonna have. *Whoosh*—out with the uterus! It had served its purpose and was now just taking up space. (And that was space needed for what, exactly? Change for the drink machine? Extra mittens?)

I was with my mother just the other day at one of her many different doctor visits, and the routine first-visit questionnaire revealed that she had had a hysterectomy when she was thirty-nine—thirty-nine! The doctor—a sweet young thing from California, bless her heart—asked Mama why she'd had the hysterectomy, and Mama just looked blank and said, "Well, mercy! I don't know! The doctor just said I needed one." I explained to the little doctor girl how it used to be. She was astounded. I informed her that she'd be hard-pressed to find more than maybe a half-dozen uteri over the age of seventy in the South—if the women possessing those uteri lived all of their lives down here. Used to be around here, you had to run off to parts unknown to hang on to *your* parts.

But the tales the women told of menopause—lordhelp-usall—again they came with the graphic descriptions. I can remember when I was about ten—I know I had not started my period yet, and after this, I was terrified of the thing—the latest neighborhood hysterectomy was being discussed over coffee at my mama's kitchen table. The woman who was about to go under the knife (Southern women of a certain age never "have surgery," they "go under the knife"—it sounds more exciting) was weaving the tale of how it came to be. It seems that her periods had become irregular and then one fine day, with no apparent warning, she commenced to hemorrhaging and she commenced it in the macaroni aisle at the Jitney-Jungle grocery store. "I was just standing there," she explained, "going through my coupons—you know, the paper had a fifteen-cent coupon on Chef Boyardee—and I reached up to get a can, and all of a sudden, *my shoes filled up with blood!*" Now, at first I had no idea what had happened to her—her *shoes* filled up with blood? This was a foot issue we were covering? After a few more gag-inducing details from the hapless victim, I realized that the blood had coursed downward and landed in her shoes. I wanted to run screaming from the room to avoid hearing any more of this macabre story, but I was mesmerized by her voice: "And I just had to leave my cart full of groceries—ice cream and all, just a-meltin'—and walk to my car, my feet just squishin' blood out of my shoes every step of the way. It looked like they'd slaughtered a hog right there in the Jitney and just dragged it out and put it in my car. And don't you just know, it was Double Coupon Day, and I missed it."

Now, regarding all those *"perhaps* unnecessary" hysterectomies, let me just say that if you've ever lived through any variety of "female" cancer, either your own or that of someone dear to you, it gives you pause. You find yourself wishing that you, or they, could have *had* one of those jobs sooner than you or they did. I swore a holy oath to my precious friend Cindy, who is just worn slap out with cancer, that if any doctor, anywhere, anytime expressed the *remotest* interest in the removal of my uterus, I would yank it out myself and hand it to him on the spot—no delay and no questions asked. As someone personally dealing right this very moment with a potential breast cancer diagnosis waiting in the wings, and having lived through the real deal with countless friends, some surviving, some not, I can tell you that if there's a hint of anything that looks like it might even *think* about turning into cancer, they can have my tits and give me some new ones—or not. Tits do not equate with life, unless you are currently being breast-fed. (If you've had any suspicious parts, I beg you, get whatever second and third opinions you want, but don't delay treatment. This concludes the lecture. [My report was good, by the way.] Proceed with the nonsense!)

Food is also a major topic of discussion at these sacred womanly gatherings. Food and diets—specifically, which foods can you eat on which diet, and who has lost how much while following it. The more bizarre the diet, the more likely it is that we will try it: "Nothing but pink weenies and ice cream." "Eat anything you want but drink apple cider vinegar in water with every meal." "Exercise all day long, and sleep less than four hours a night—you'll be too tired to chew." "Eat nothing that has a face or a mother." "Nothing that grows in dirt, but bacon galore!" Let me just say that if you want to lose weight, you're probably going to have to give up on the idea of "galore!" anything. Although, admittedly, "galore!" is one of our very favorite food groups. Truth be told, we adore "galore!" in just about any context.

Since we are the Queens of Wretched Excess, the diet discussions usually take place *while* we're eating at the party. We'll have a little luncheon plate stacked four or five layers deep with enough calorie power to fuel a team of sled dogs through a blizzard, but we will *insist* on diet drinks and artificially sweetened tea—just to show that we are not completely oblivious to dietary concerns. After the diet discussion/Big Feed, we all write down the recipes for all the fattening stuff we just ate because we want to be able to eat it again, at will, in our own homes: Calories do not attach if no one witnesses you in the act of consuming them—this is common knowledge.

And then we talk about plastic surgery. Who's had what hiked up, tucked in, sucked out, augmented, downsized, or otherwise altered? Who did the work? How does it look? What did it cost? Is she going out yet and is it a secret? Interesting that the "secret" part of the discussion comes at the end—after all the information has been shared, dissected, and devoured—so it's pretty much moot by then, I'd say, but we ask just the same.

Lots of people want it to be a secret. I don't understand that. For one thing, everybody can *tell*. I mean, last month you were flat as a pancake, but now your chest turns the corner before you do, and that's, what, a lucky fluke? Last month your neck looked like a turkey gobbler, and today it's skinned back tighter than the devil's hatband and you're short a few dozen moles—and nobody's supposed to question that? The bags under your eyes were so big you looked like you were peeking up over a rock, but all of a sudden you show up looking like one of those portraits of the little kids with the big eyes? And Botox—please! Your face is *paralyzed*. Do you think we don't notice? You can't frown—which is not very handy, because there are so many people in the world who need to be frowned at, a lot. If you can't do your part, the rest of us will have to double up and frown at them twice as much, which is not particularly hard, but neither is it fair for us to carry your load just so you can look bland and unwrinkled. And why would anybody want to look bland? "Make me look like a blank-slate, permanent poker face, with not a thought in my head"? It's beyond me. But anyway, if you've been frowning along pretty well for the last elevendy years or so and you show up one day looking like the "after" girl in a douche ad, we all know you either had Botox or you're heavily medicated. And we really don't care—just don't lie to us. We aren't stupid.

The point is, everybody knows—they always know. If you try to keep it a secret, that just 100 percent guarantees you'll be the topic of the day at every gahh-den club in town, to say nothing of the break room where you work. My theory has always been that whatever you do, just tell it. Blab it to whoever will stand still to listen. What fun is it to gossip about you if you yourself put the shit out there first? If we're not getting away with something by repeating it behind your back—well, all the joy just goes right out of it.

So with that in mind—*Hey! I had a face-lift this summer!* In *The Big-Ass Cookbook (and Financial Planner)*, I told about having had my eyes done. Well, that went so well, I have pretty much adopted plastic surgery as my hobby. I decided that there was no point in my eyes looking all wide-awake and all if the rest of my face looked like it was ready to crawl off in the bushes and die, so I betook myself to the Hills of Bever-lee and signed up with Dr. Harry Glassman (who is married to Victoria Principal, which is apropos of nothing—or maybe it is) and got him to assess the damage of my fifty years of grinning directly into the face of the sun. I have long aspired to having bigger tits, as you know, and so my plan was to have a "twofer." As long as I'm there and out cold, just fix everything.

If there's one thing that women have been led to believe is a prerequisite for attracting and keeping the man of our dreams, it's large and perfect breasts. And boy-hidee, did we luck out here, because I am here to tell you a fact: They're makin' them thangs ever' day! There's hardly a town in this country where you can't just about run out on your lunch hour and come back to work with a shiny new set of big'uns. We can get some big tits if we want them, by God, and I've been talking about doing that very thing for just about as long as I can remember— certainly ever since I first got my real ones. They have never been particularly satisfactory—never what you'd call "cute," certainly not perky, not even when they were brand-new. It's kinda like maybe I got a used set by mistake, y'know? And I was just *this* close to getting a new set once, and for some reason I couldn't explain, I changed my mind at the last minute and didn't do it. I've always been glad because years later I had my precious baby daughter, BoPeep, and I wouldn't have missed breast-feeding her for a million billion dollars. But now—well, now would actually be a pretty good time to get them at least hiked up. And as long as we're hiking 'em up, we might as well go on and augment, right? And my theory has always been: If you're gonna get some, get 'em bigger'n your head.

So I was thinking, How great will *this* be? I can go out of town for a couple of weeks and come back with the face and other pertinent parts of a twenty-five-year-old! Of course, I would still have a fifty-year-old ass, but hey, I'm working from the top down here.

Alas, it was not to be.

With more tact than I would have believed possible under the circumstances, Dr. Glassman communicated to me that he could do one or the other but not both at the same time, because it was way too big a job. That struck me and Tammy (who naturally had accompanied me on my quest) as unbearably funny, in a cruel-joke-at-my-expense kind of way, and we laughed hysterically at it, to Dr. Glassman's great discomfort. I got the feeling that he's not accustomed to a whole lot of his normal Hollywood clientele laughing at their saggy old selves. So anyway, I had to prioritize my procedures, and I decided that the face and neck situation was much more urgent than the one in my bra. Even though it's been my observation that if your tits are big enough, nobody much notices anything else for a pretty good while, I myself spend more time looking at my face than I do at my tits, so I decided to go for the face. And the neck. Can you even believe what happens to your neck when you cruise around those mid-forties? How is that possible?

It was decided, after much lifting and looking at various parts of my face, that I needed what is called in plastic surgery terms the Whole Shebang. Other than my nose, all of my facial parts had headed south and all would be lassoed and hauled back up where they belonged. Dr. William Fein, noted ophthalmologist, would be called in to correct one of my eyes: One was saggier than the other, and when I was tired, it would, naturally, sag even more, causing the wider-open one to resemble nothing so much as a large brown *glass* eye.

A lot of calendar coordinating followed on account of we had to accommodate Dr. Glassman's and Dr. Fein's schedules, as well as mine, and then, of course, the Cutest Boy in the World *insisted* on going with me to provide me with round-the-clock ice packs and whatever else I might need at whatever moment I might need it, and naturally Tammy wanted to come out so we could play and shop during my recovery. And possibly she would have "a little something" done at the same time—just to be folksy. (We put a high premium on group outings: Just last year, after we turned fifty, we went dutifully out and had our recommended colonoscopies—together. Katie Couric said to, and we like to be in accordance with Katie, don't you?)

At last we settled on a week in June that was perfect for the schedules of all concerned . . . so of course I got bronchitis. Probably the very last thing you want to do much of after you've just had your entire face basically peeled like a grape, hunks of it lopped off, and then the revised edition stuck back on, is cough. I was coughing hard and doing plenty of it, so all of the calendars had to be re-consulted and we came up with a time in August.

If you're going to leave Mississippi for a couple of weeks, August is about the best time to do it, unless you like to sweat and swat mosquitoes. L.A. is a good place to go because it's rarely as hot and they've never even heard of mosquitoes. (When they heard the word, they thought it was some kind of new pointy-toed shoe that one of those Jimmy Choo guys was making.)

So here we go, out to Beverly Hills, me and Tammy and the Cutest Boy in the World, only something got confused (him) and he didn't come out until late the next day, and by then I had already been Under the Knife. When we had parted at the Jackson airport, I looked like my regular (old) self. By the time he got to L.A., my entire head was encased in a big giant bandage, and the parts showing were "all swole up" and festooned with black and blue stitches. There were two *Phillips-head screws* in the top of my head—really. You couldn't actually see them, but just hearing they were in there gave him that last little push—right on over the edge. I had a lovely suite in one of these places they have all over Beverly Hills where you go recuperate from plastic surgery. They have nurses on duty round the clock to fetch you drugs and ice bags and Jell-O and mashed potatoes. Since I had a big ole suite, Tammy and the Cutest Boy in the World were staying with me. They had a large time and entertained themselves and each other in all manner of ways that remain unknown to me because I was completely zonked out on drugs most all of the time. Now, let me tell you, when somebody gives you Xanax, Vicodin, and Ambien, you will flat sleep—even if they did just rip your face off.

The next day, Tammy had her "little procedure" and moved into the adjoining room, and so then Cutie Pie had two dreamboats to look at and after. The day after that, we moved out of the hospital/hotel and into a regular hotel, which was Le Meridien on account of the superdeep bathtubs, don't you know. We had also gotten their room service menu in advance and determined that there was a sufficient number of items containing cheese to meet our anticipated needs.

The Cutest Boy in the World stayed up all night for about six nights in a row, changing our ice packs, rearranging pillows, and telling us how much he loved us. I don't recall that he was actually *looking* at us when he said it, however. The last night he was there, Tammy and I had ordered room service—I had the big giant bandage off but was still not exactly what you'd call "presentable"—and Cutie Pie pulled the old "I'll be right back" scheme. He disappeared for several hours. We found out later he was just downstairs in the bar, and he came back completely blind, shit-faced drunk and launched into a semi-loud sob fest. We finally deciphered from his snuffling and blubbering that he was afraid the current state of my face was going to somehow be permanent, and that the prospect was distressing to him because he *loved* my former face and had not perceived it to be flawed in the least. At least that's what we think he was saying. It actually sounded more like "Uhhhhuuuhuhhh—you' faaaae [snuffle/blubber]. Ha cuh yew dooo tha t' yo' faaaae [tone going up at the end, implying a question]? Ah lub yo lil faaaae— ple-e-e-e- ple-e-e-e ple-e-e-e don evuh do nuffiness to yo lil faaaaae [much snuffling, blubbering, and wiping his nose on his sleeve]."

We decided it was just too much for him. The next day we overheard him on the phone talking to one of the Queens' husbands back in Jackson. "If she wants to do it, man, get Jill to go with her and help her—a husband just does *not* need to see this, I'm telling you. We'll fuckin' go to Europe, man. You do *not* want to see what I've seen this week." Bless his heart. We'll see if he's that sensitive when I go get my tits done.

Anyway, Tammy and I remained in L.A. for another week, going out daily on small shopping excursions. This entertained us and also provided enough exercise for us to regain our strength for the long flight home. Lemme tell you, a couple weeks lying around taking drugs and ordering room service just takes it out of you, and gentle periods of gratuitous shopping are needed to restore one's verve—and I was in bad need of a sackful of verve. Purse and shoe shopping are excellent post-face-lift exercises because attention to either item directs one's gaze away from one's face. One hardly ever holds a shoe or a purse up to one's face to see how one likes it. There is the added benefit that the size of one's ass does not in any way determine the fit of a shoe or the suitability of a purse. If one has just spent a screaming fortune on one's face, one does not, at that particular time, need to be reminded that one's ass is the size of the sun.

So we'd go out, totter around shopping a bit, and then hop in a cab and head back to the hotel, practically disrobing in the elevator, so great was our haste to be back in our jammies. Tammy's room was our dining room. She would order our cheese and fried items, and I would lay out our drugs and prepare my room—which had two beds—for our afternoon rest. After we ate our cheesy/fried things and took our drugs, we'd get in our beds and watch Dr. Phil until we drifted off. Then we'd wake up and have tea and decide which cheesy/fried things we'd order for dinner. It was the best vacation we ever had— and talk about coming home looking rested!

By the time we flew home, we could put on makeup, and although our faces were still a little swollen, unless you *knew*, you'd never know—y'know? I'm telling you, my own mother, who lives with me, could not tell and, to this day, does not know that I had a face-lift! Unless she makes it to the end of this book, she never will know. That is how good Drs. Glassman and Fein are, and that's just about the highest recommendation I could give. (That and the fact that their nurses and staff are all Queenly, and you know how important that is.) Before I went, a good friend of mine said, "Honey, don't mess around askin' for that 'well-rested' look." She'd had several rounds of that and it always needed redoing before she could turn around, she explained. "What I'm goin' for next time around is, every time I walk into a room, I want somebody to say to their girlfriend, 'Damn! Look at *her!* Girl, now, *that* is some fine plastic surgery right there!'" I guess I see her point, but I really didn't want to look permanently surprised or like I'm fighting the urge to grimace or have even the more moderate my-ponytail-is-just-a-lit-tle-too-tight look.

Don't be shy. If you see me at a book signing or something, you can ask me about it—I have no pride. I will tell you everything.

Having plastic surgery is one of the more drastic things we'll do for love. And it really is done for other people. Yes, it's my face, and yes, it drives me crazy that it's falling down, but if the rest of the world was blind, would I be paying out the ying-yang to have it hiked up? I won't say that I doubt it, because I am absolutely certain I would not be doing it. I'm pretty sure I'd be spending that money on trashy books and chocolate. It wouldn't even have to be the entire rest of the world that was blind, and not even all the men—just *my* man. My precious darlin' childhood friends, Harry and Margaret, each have a problem that might cause weeping and wailing and gnashing of teeth in lesser mortals: Harry is losing his sight and Margaret has thinning hair. The two, who've been lovebirds for all but the first twelve years of their lives, have really the only workable attitude possible, since apparently nothing can be done to remedy either problem: They just laugh and say they hope Harry goes blind before Margaret goes bald. Love. It.

Now, the Cutest Boy in the World is practically blind when he takes his glasses off, and I do think that explains a lot about our relationship. He does see really well with his glasses *on*, however, so as I see it, I really had no choice about this face-lift thing. If he wants to dissuade me from future repair jobs, I will just have to poke his eyes out—that's all I'm saying.

And since having my "work done," I regularly encounter people who seem to think it's some kind of *moral* choice. Some women smile "sweetly" and say that *they* will not be having any plastic surgery. "I have *earned* this face, these wrinkles" is the standard line. Hmmmm. How to respond to such holiness? Health nuts love to tell us how we wouldn't put fuel in our car as crappy as what we put in our bodies, but it's not okay to fix up the outside? Everybody paints their house from time to time or the homeowners' association would have their hide—and every man I ever loved was willing to spend thousands of dollars at the auto body shop to repair the tiniest, nearly invisible scratch or dent on a car that they wouldn't have for more than another two years tops. But it's somehow *wrong* to fix the face that I have to look out from behind every day of my entire life?

I generally smile "sweetly" and say nothing, but I can't help thinking: Well, as it happens, I not only earned my own wrinkles, I also earned the money to pay for having them removed! I also notice quite frequently that these same women don't share the same sense of loyalty to their gray hair as they do to their wrinkles, since they're oh so regular about staying *blond.* Count me in with Dolly Parton, who looks at plastic surgery as a lifetime maintenance program. When something sags, hike it up; when something needs nipping, nip it; and by golly, tuck that sucker if it needs tucking—if you want to. And if you don't want to, hey, that's okay, too. Nobody has an owner's covenant declaring that you have to keep up the property to suit anybody else.

# 9

## Enhancements Galore!

Massive amounts of money are spent every year convincing women that men want us to be—or at least look—young, with big, pouty lips (now, there's something I've never understood—who's ever been attracted to a person who was pouting?), enormous breasts, and a massive head full of preternaturally shining hair. As you may recall from prior perusals of my pages, the distribution of hair has not been fair and equitable among the ranks of the Sweet Potato Queens, and there is no middle ground. This is truly a matter of the Haves and the Have Nots. I place myself in the latter group, and I can tell you, there is no small amount of backbiting over this issue. They have hair, we don't, and we hate them for it. We hate their hairy guts for it. We wish *we* had their hair and they had something awful instead—like maybe *our* hair. That would teach them.

All our pathetic attempts at hair augmentation have failed miserably. There is no product at any price (believe me, we've paid plenty) that can deliver any relief, real or imagined. If our four hairs each were the biblical loaves and fishes, the Five Thousand would just have to fill up on water; there is no follicular miracle out there for the likes of us. Many are the promises of the myriad balms and unguents—fine, thin, limp, wispy locks transformed before your very eyes into abundant, thick, bouncy, *enviable* hair, glorious hair. You might just as well slather that stuff on a frog—it would probably do him as much good as it's done us. Sigh.

Then we heard about weaves and extensions—actual big hair somehow semipermanently and undetectably attached to our own few hairs. We gazed with unvarnished envy at the hair on the heads of some of our friends, hair that had been bought at the hair store and attached to their own by various means. It looked so good we could not stand it. We were somewhat taken aback by how the stuff felt, though. Oh, it feels fine on top, but if you feel underneath—YOWZA! I can't even tell you what it feels like under there, but it feels reeeeally bad—millions and millions of little knotty-feeling things. You can absolutely forget about having anybody (including your ownself) run their fingers through your beautiful hair. This was momentarily off-putting to us because, of course, a large part of the pleasure of hair is having it manhandled by actual men, but the lure of the Big Hair was just too strong for us. We were willing to spend the rest of our romantic lives dodging anyone's attempt at touching our heads, not unlike guys who wear toupees. (You know what that maneuver looks like if you've ever been out with a rug-top guy. Your hand gets anywhere near that head and he's swooping backward and sideways. He has some kind of weird radar for when a hand is approaching that hairpiece, and his body reacts automatically to prevent contact.) We went so far as to have a consultation and we were assured by the hair woman that yes, indeed, we could leave her shop that very *day* with a big fine head of hair. And we nearly took the plunge, but something made us consult our own personal hair guy first. He looked at us as if we'd asked if he thought we should shave off our eye-brows. Yes, indeed, we *could*, in fact, march our little nappy-headed selves right back down to that hair woman and get ourselves some Very Big Hair that she would glue or tie or otherwise affix to our puny little baby hairs, and in no time at all we would be completely bald, on account of all that big hair would pull our puny little baby hairs out by their puny little baby roots. And, he said, if you think you're miserable with your hair now, just imagine how you'll feel when you have to go back to having four hairs after having very briefly had Big Hair. Of course, it'll take so long to grow those four hairs back, you'll probably be pretty glad to have 'em. Yes, on second thought, maybe that's just the thing y'all need to do—cultivate a little gratitude. We slunk away, muttering under our breath at him, but we did not succumb to the hair woman's temptations.

Or at least not *that* hair woman. We, uh, found another one who made us feel that big, safe hair was within our grasp, and so we forked over a fairly large pile of money and we each received our very own custom-matched—I don't know what the official name is, but what it looks like to us is a hair pie, like a cow pie, only hair. It's a little flat circle of hair and you tie it on your head and then you pull your own hair through the spaces (hair holes) and comb it all together and take off the little tie thingee and *voy-ola*, instant Big Hair that is held safely on top of your head by your very own hair. That's the theory, anyway. And it probably works good, too—for people with big, thick hair that's easy to grab hold of and pull through the hair holes, but those people don't need any more hair, and for *us*— well, it just didn't work at all. That's because the hair pie completely smashes our four little hairs and holds them tight against our heads so you can't get hold of enough hairs to pull 'em through, and the hair pie is always slipping off to one side or crawling off the back of your head in a decidedly furtive manner, which does not render a good look at all, as you might imagine. It was a good idea—on paper—and not so good on our actual heads, but at least it left only our wallets bare and not our actual heads. Then we saw the exact same thing in a catalog for twenty bucks—I swear. It's just terrible the way we, the nearly hairless, are preyed upon by unscrupulous hair vendors.

Bad hair is not the only affliction visited upon us—we've also got no lips, pouty or otherwise. And yes, the Queens with the Big Hair also got the big lips, or at least lips. The rest of us got chicken lips. As I previously rambled, chickens don't have teeth; well, they are also lipless, in case you hadn't noticed, although how could you not? And so it was that as the fiftieth birthday of one of the Queens approached—Tammy turned fifty!—I found myself, as I often do, sitting on a plane on a taxiway in Atlanta for about three days, waiting to take off or land—who can tell anymore? Having read everything with real writing in it in the entire cabin, I was reduced to scanning the *SkyMall* to pass the time. And there it was: the Lip Enhancer! Full, luscious, succulent, lip-smackin' lips were guaranteed from using the Lip Enhancer for only a few seconds at a time—and they would last for weeks! With no hesitation whatsoever, I tore the page from the *SkyMall*, and as soon as the use of cell phones was permitted, I dialed 'em up and gave 'em my credit-card number, ordering no fewer than four Lip Enhancers to be shipped to me without delay.

Now, the birthday was some weeks away, and so I had the great good fun of taunting not only Tammy but also Tammy and Tammy (together we are the Lip-Free Gang of Four) with maddening hints about the upcoming birthday and my celebratory plans for same. I told them they could plan whatever they wanted for whatever crowd they chose, but one night had to be reserved for a very private gathering of the Four. Tammy was suspicious and disgruntled. She repeatedly demanded to know if it involved taking our clothes off, and I said, "Omigod, *no*." (I understood without discussion the reason for her panicked query. As you know, matter is never lost in the universe, and that certainly includes body weight. If one person loses, the next one gains, and as it happened at that particular juncture of time, Tammy and Tammy had somehow contrived to *lose* a number of pounds, which meant, of course, that Tammy and I had *gained* them, so I assured her that, even though our gatherings did not normally include bouts of nudity anyway, there for sure would not be any *this* time.) I drove them all fairly wild with my daily phone calls filled with mysterious references to the upcoming soiree, always ending with a dictum of dire secrecy: "It's only for the Four." What could this be that required the banishment not only of boys but of our other Queens as well?

By the time the day of the event finally arrived, I had compulsively ordered any number of other items from the lip service industry, and so I set at each of our places an enormous cardboard box, which was filled with several other cardboard boxes of assorted sizes and shapes. In those boxes were lip liners, lip goo, lip shine, lip color that was guaranteed to stay on forever until you took it off with what smelled and felt like paint thinner—and the ultimate body-shaping device of the universe: the Lip Enhancer. Many delighted shrieks emitted from our happy non-lips as we each tore open the main package and beheld the clear plastic cylinder, lying there benignly in its fuzzy blue pre-molded box.

"What the fuck *is* it?" they asked admiringly.

"It'll give us big lips," I offered in explanation. This remark was met with deafening squeals of glee, as you might imagine, the air screaming out of the stretched balloon-tops that are our mouths. Fortunately, I had opened mine at home, and so at least *somebody* had read the instructions. Not *me*, of course. The Cutest Boy in the World had read them and told me what they said. Queens do not ever read the instructions—we *give* the instructions. So I instructed them: It's a suction thingee—you put your mouth in one end and you pull the plunger thingee out the other end, slowly, and then you hold it there. It's kind of like when you were a kid and would suck on a Coke bottle until it sucked back and your lips went down into the bottleneck and you could actually walk around with the Coke bottle hanging off your lips until you moved your tongue and released the vacuum. Pretty cool—go try it now if this childhood exercise escaped you, and you can also use it instead of ordering the Lip Enhancer from the *SkyMall* catalog, because that's all it does. Well, except that a whole lot more mouth will fit in this plastic tube than will fit in a Coke bottleneck. I do seem to recall Cutie Pie maybe saying that the instructions were pretty clear that you needed to be careful and sort of ease into regular use of the Lip Enhancer. I didn't really remember that right off the bat, but I did tell the others just the very second I did remember. But it probably wouldn't have made any difference to Tammy, anyway.

Our Tammy is a tad on the competitive side. She always gives 110 percent—even when 25 percent is about 15 percent too much. You've no doubt heard that "winning isn't everything." *You* have heard that but Tammy has not, because if you try to say it to her, she slams her hands over her ears and goes, "Dip-dip-dip-dip-dip-dip-dip-dip," real loud until she thinks you're through. It's not really that Tammy enjoys winning so much as she just loves beating the crap out of others. And so it was that, despite any warnings to the contrary, Tammy shoved her little lip-starved mouth down in that tube and she yanked back on that plunger and she held *firm*, and she held firm for a long, long time—way past the time when the rest of us pussies had quit and were picking ourselves up off the floor, laughing and looking at each other's "enhanced" lips and laughing some more. Chicken Shit Tammy had been way too—well, the name says it all—to even try very hard, while Birthday Tammy had actually achieved some discernible lips for the first time ever, and I managed to cause a shocking engorgement not only of my upper lip but also of the area directly above my lip and beneath my nose, giving me an odd monkeyish air. The three of us were laughing way too hard to hold any kind of suitable suction, but not ole Blood and Guts Tammy. She was grim-faced and determined—iron grip on both tube and plunger—and as we turned our gaze upon her, we saw that this was one time she'd gotten a little more than she'd bargained for. Her actual lips were remarkably unchanged; instead, all the suction had apparently been focused on the space between her lip and nose. Where I had created a monkey lip, Tammy had created a giant purple throbbing *hickey*. I'm telling you, this thing was *fine!* It was *way* big and of a purple color that was both deep and bright—a true royal purple, I'd call it. You could see that thing when you passed her in the *car.* Of course, this all occurred on a Sunday night, making for an amusing Monday-morning staff meeting at work. I gave her my Chanel green stick—you know, the concealer that will absolutely hide *anything . . .* except, it turns out, a giant purple hickey on your upper lip. Without the green stick, she looked a whole lot like Hitler from across the room. With it, she looked like she'd just been enjoying the shit out of a bottle of grape juice. The Lip Enhancer's ad copy did not lie—the effects did last for more than a week for ole Tammy, and of course, we are all *still* enjoying it.

Then, a few weeks later was Blood and Guts Tammy's birthday, and I phoned and asked her did she want a birthday cake and she said, "Uh-huh," and I said what kind, and she said, "Birthday cake," and I asked did she want writing on it, and she said, "Uh-huh, but just my name and no *h.*" I'm wondering, Does she really think I might accidentally put an *h* in "Tammy" for some reason? And this was a small mystery for a while until I figured out that she'd actually said, "No *age,*" but by then, I was pretty carried away with the "no *h*" thing, and so I ordered her a birthday cake and had "APPY BIRTDAY, Tammy" written on it, which was not all that easy to explain to the birthday cake baker. For Tammy's "birtday"—knowing that the whole lip subject was still pretty sore, as was her actual lip—we took the high road and just had wax lips for everybody. And a pair of bunny ears for Tammy.

So then we all went Mystic Bowling, which, if you don't

know, is just like regular bowling, only you do it in the dark with black lights, which is a huge improvement on the whole thing if you ask me. There is just not enough of the mystic in this life, in my opinion, and if I can get a little at the bowling alley, then sign my ass up. So we all piled into the bowling alley and rented our shoes. Now, up until that time, I had never actually been bowling my ownself. I had taken children bowling, or at least I had taken children to a bowling alley, but I had not ever set foot in the place with the intent of personally hurling big balls across the room. And so I didn't fully understand the whole shoe thing, and in case you're similarly ignorant, they will not let you bowl without bowling *shoes,* and since if you haven't dedicated your life to bowling there's not much likelihood you'll show up with the right footwear, that means you will have to wear theirs, and you are hardly the first to do so.

There are few things in life, in my opinion, with a cringe-and-gag factor to rival that of putting rented shoes on one's personal feet. I found that I really did have to just suspend disbelief to even bring myself to do it. I had to empty my mind completely and disassociate myself from the task at hand, but somehow the shoes got on my feet and I never looked at them or acknowledged their existence in any way. I imagined—much later, when the evening was over and my feet were safe in their rightful shoes—what would have happened if, while wearing the rented shoes, I allowed myself to *know* it. I get images of myself shrieking uncontrollably and dancing about as if barefoot on hot coals, or as if perhaps I had glanced down and realized I was inexplicably standing shoeless in a sea of slugs—in any event, much yowling and flailing would ensue.

I pretty much sucked at bowling, but I was in excellent company. At least I could say it was my virgin bowling experience. My cohorts had apparently been frequenting bowling alleys off and on for their entire lives and they did not bowl noticeably better than I did. We were distinguished not only by our lousy bowling but also by the copious quantities of glow-in-the-dark makeup and jewelry with which we were ornamented. Oh, and did I mention we were all wearing wax lips? I'm here to tell you, everybody looks good—if not better—in a set of wax lips, and I have got the photos to prove it. Yes, you look pretty cute in wax lips, and while you're wearing them it's hard to say anything you'll regret later, on account of it's nearly impossible to say anything at all, so you can forget about even making, let alone delivering on the Promise (which for some would be the main selling point right there). The main drawback is that you absolutely cannot eat or drink while wearing them, but they're hard to beat for sheer good looks. Put some on you and your friends and take your picture and see for yourself. Not what you'd call your pouty lips, now, but pretty cute, yessireebob, pret-ty dang cute.

Now, I personally have not ever had one single guy in my whole lifelong experience with guys ever say to my face that he wished I had bigger hair, tits, or lips. These are just things that women get told by magazines that men are dying for us to have, and we decide, based on nothing but this hearsay, to believe it. Fine. My own personal experience with guys has been that whatever it is that you've got, they will be just absolutely tickled to *death* with it if you give them any kind of access to it at all. They are not nearly as critical of us as we are, and it's a damn good thing, too—nobody would *ever* get any if they were.

One of the Queens, Tammy, did have a guy who expressed a mild interest in the Brazilian wax craze that was ripping through the country a while back, so she went and got one as a special surprise homecoming happy for him. (Let me pause for a moment here and note that men do not ever consider yanking out their body hair—not any of it—for our entertainment, pleasure, or convenience. It simply never occurs to them. Even if it looks like they're wearing a fur jacket underneath when they take their shirt off, do they fret and race off to the waxing salon? They do not. If they have one giant eyebrow that takes up most of what on most other primates would be considered "forehead," do they pluck out the offending hairs? Only if they have wives lying in wait with the tweezers. We once knew a girl whose guy read way too many guy magazines—like the ones that tell guys little tricks to do to make their penii look larger. Oh, please. Yes, he read it. He believed it. And he did it. He took manicure scissors and *trimmed* his pubic hair, the theory being that the shorter hair would give the illusion of big or at least bigger. Wrong. So very, very, *very* wrong. She assured him that no, it did not have the desired effect of making anything look bigger, but even if it did, that would never counteract the other effect that it had, and that would be doing a bang-up job of making him look like an idiot, and an idiot who had sat around with manicure scissors, fiddling with his parts. This activity, she assured him, was many times worse than the time he got the hair on his head *frosted*. [That was the last time she had any interest in viewing any of his parts, including his face.] We really do like our guys to be guylike and worry about the air pressure in our tires and stuff like that—*not* going to the beauty shop and sitting around in a little cape, getting their hair foil-wrapped and tinted, and certainly not engaging in furtive activities involving manicure scissors.)

But anyway, back to the guy for whom Tammy got the Big Wax. I think it's fair to say that he was surprised and happy enough that she was not sorry she'd gone to the trouble. And it *was* some trouble, let me tell you. Over the years, I guess we've all had our share of bikini waxes, eyebrow shapings, and lip rips, but Tammy assures us that none of those in any way prepares you for the utterly daunting task of yanking out all of one's pubic hair. And it's the kind of thing that you really can't grasp the magnitude of until you're really sort of *committed*, you know. You've pretty much *got* to go on with the thing and try not to be, if you'll excuse the expression, a complete pussy about it. Because Tammy reports that it does evermore *hurt*— and besides, it is not a dignified process. Talk about your bizarre bonding experience—it's not easy to keep up any pretense of pride with your service provider when she's putting hot wax on your hoo-hoo and yanking out all the hair thereon. Tammy's dedicated service provider asked her, between yanks and yowls, if she was doing this for her husband. Through clenched teeth, Tammy replied, "Hunny, I have never had a *husband* I would do *this* for. I've had a few I would have happily done it *to*, but no, ma'am, certainly not *for*." And the wax lady just laughed and laughed and swore *that* was the pure truth, which it was.

So, of course, women being women—meaning that we will tell absolutely anything to our girlfriends—yes, Tammy told, and no, it wasn't enough for them just to hear about it. They wanted to *see* it, and so it was that for a period of several weeks, Tammy's nearest and dearest girlfriends, no matter where they were—like outside on the walking track at the Y—called upon her to provide just the tiniest peek at Slick. Yes, hunny, we will do just about anything for love, but rest assured, we *are* gonna talk about it.

And let me just say that so far in our lives, none of us ever had a man do *anything* that I would call even the near-equivalent of the Brazilian wax Tammy got for love. . . . Okay, so I may have been a little hasty with that last sentence—I completely forgot about my friend Heather's experience. Skunk season had hit particularly hard at Heather's house; there were no fewer than five of them living under her house. A popular method of deskunkification at the time was to sling a few handfuls of mothballs under there with 'em. Well, Heather did that, and what does the village skunk idiot do but *eat* one and fall over dead right in front of her. She was happy it was dead but not looking forward to the prospect of having to deal with the carcass. Enter the New and Absolutely Wonderful New Husband. He immediately bags the beast and vows to "dispose" of it later. A few days went by before she thought to ask him what exactly he had done with the body. And what he did will surely elevate him to sainthood. Heather had not only this New and Absolutely Wonderful New Husband but also a real jackass of a rat bastard *ex*-husband who'd been making life difficult for her, and so what did this precious newbie do? He sacked up that dead skunk and took it right over to the ex-husband's winterized boat and just slid it right under the cover and left it where it would be safe and sound for the next few months. And that right there is what you call your True Love.

# 10

## Shock and Awe

Absolutely the only thing in the entire universe, living or dead, that will make me *not* hungry is total obsession over a guy. I've been known to drop fifteen to twenty actual pounds. Believe me, nothing else that I have so far encountered in this life produces that effect on my person—not Watching Weight, not Busting Sugar. There is simply no shrinking Zone for me except for a *man*.

One of the Queens, Tammy, went to Weight Watchers—or WW, as she calls it—for a brief spell. She actually lost weight (as does anybody who really works that program, because it is safe, healthy, effective, and doable). As a matter of fact, she would be slim and trim this very day if it wasn't for her friends—that would be us, of course. She told us that WW taught, "Nothing tastes as good as being thin feels." And we all agreed that is the gospel truth. Being thin would *feel so good*. But we aren't thin. And we suck at delaying gratification.

A couple of the Tammys and I have spent many hours— sometimes happy, sometimes torturous—and many miles in the early mornings on the track at our YMCA, walking and talking, and the subjects of conversation rarely vary: Sex. Food. How fat we are. And infinite variations and combinations of those themes. As in: All we want is sex, but we're too fat to *do* it, let alone allow anybody to *see* us, so we might as well eat something. And off we go to the Waffle House across the high-way for a little something scattered, smattered, flattered, and fried, where we continue the conversation, over breakfast, about how fat we are, who all we might sleep with if we were not so fat, and should we get the waffles, too? "Why not?" is the usual reply.

Many people, including and probably most especially *us*, have wondered from time to time how it is that we can walk so very much and yet still be so very fat. I finally concluded that we are suffering from what I call Fat Mailman Syndrome. Like the occasional chubby mailman you'll see out pounding the pavement, our bodies are so very much accustomed to the route, distance, and pace we maintain each day that it just doesn't even count as exercise anymore. We—and that chubby mailman—need to do something to increase the intensity of our workout, like running, skipping, and/or jumping, but really, I don't see it happening for any of us. We'd rather whine.

Tammy Donna, our quesopigeterian dieter (quesopigeterians eat a moderate amount of lettuce with gobs of cheese and cheese-based salad dressings accompanied by cheese bread and sometimes bacon, but they like to *say* they're vegetarian because they think it sounds mysterious, and frankly, it is—I mean, how anybody could or would even want to live without bacon is a major mystery to me), subsists almost entirely on cheese, sweet tea with lemon, and carbohydrates of the lowest order, and she's continually baffled by the scales. I understand and share her bafflement: I eat regularly and largely from the Official Four Food Groups of the Sweet Potato Queens—those being Sweet, Salty, Fried, and Au Gratin—and yet I gaze with shock and awe at the ever-climbing numbers on my weighing apparatus.

Recently I found an acupuncturist who agreed to perform weight-loss-inducing needle tricks on us. Did it matter that we had to pay him large sums of money—in cash—and drive ninety miles one way for the privilege of being human pin cushions? You know it did not. Here's the scene: We would alternate whose car we took because, according to the doctor, neither of us was supposed to drive after the procedure—this way, we each cut in half the risk we were taking. But, of course, we could not *admit* to another living soul what we were doing, which would have been necessary to get someone to drive us down there, so although we know there're not many things worth risking your life for, we also knew that keeping this secret was one of them. Some of you may actually ask *why*. Because (a) it was humiliating that we were so powerless over our own mouths that we were reduced to driving to one of the outlying rings of *hell* to have a stranger stick needles in our actual bodies, in a pitiful attempt to lose weight without *trying* (we weren't remotely interested in that). And perhaps even more important, (b) if it actually worked, we'd have the scoop of the century! We would be rail-thin, the envy of all, and we would say *nothing*. We'd be serenely, smugly, slyly, silently *skinny*. And all the while we could "eat like a field hand and gobble like a hawg"—which serves as sport in our Queenly domain.

The actual treatments did create a rare bonding experience. Oh, I know we women bond over margaritas and chocolate; we carry one another through all the good and bad that life throws our way, and I'm not discounting any of that. Picture it: We insisted on sharing a treatment room because we were in high hysterics over the whole thing and didn't want to miss talking about a single detail of any of it—plus Tammy Donna is a notorious chicken-shit crybaby and refused to get out of my room. No, we just mainly wanted to laugh as much as possible, and each of us thought that the sight of the other one stuck full of needles was not to be missed. Naturally, since I am the Boss Queen (and the biggest), I got the fold-out examining table, so I could lie down (although a fair amount of leg was hanging off the end). Tammy Donna had to sit bolt upright in one chair with her little legs stuck straight out in front of her, propped on another chair. Suffice it to say, nobody in the room was exactly comfy—including the hapless doctor, who found it very difficult to maneuver around all that was us in order to stick his many needles into our assorted parts. The fact that we were laughing like a couple of fat, prickly hyenas probably did not enhance the moment for him, either.

The first treatment involved needles only—and they are really and truly so tiny, it is not painful at all. Not one bit. I swear. Even the ones that went right smack between our eyes didn't hurt a bit—although they popped out quite a few times from our laughing, and he'd have to come jam 'em back in there. I know his other patients, most of whom were there for just regular ole doctoring, not acupuncture, were not a little curious about the two big ole girls wedged up in the same exam room, laughing fit to kill. But you know what? It worked! And we do not care one whit why or how. All we know is when we left there, we weren't hungry, and we weren't too very hungry for the whole next week until we went back again—and you better *believe* we went back. Hunny, whatchoo talkin' 'bout? We both lost weight and we'da crawled on our bellies like *rep*-tiles to get back down there. We would have hocked jewelry, committed minor felonies, anything short of sleeping with ex-husbands, but we were *going back.*

We breezed in, happy and offhand about it the second time—old hands at the acupuncture game, we fancied ourselves. Weighed in for the nurses—who were impressed and we knew not a little envious over our losses—went unescorted to "our" room, assumed our positions, and waited to be stuck once more. Oh yeah, we wanted it bad, baby. Come on in here and *stick* us, big boy. Well. He was forevermore ready for *us* that day. He explained that that day's treatment would be "slightly more aggressive than last week's." It seems the body builds a tolerance and must be subjected to increasingly more powerful pricks for the effect to continue and progress. Yeah, yeah, yeah, fine, bring it *on*, Doc. We're not as fat as we were when we left here last week—we are *intrepid*. Even though a couple of the sticks did prove to be on a groan- and/or gasp-producing level, we ultimately laughed even harder and went on off back home, with a much-welcomed loss of appetite. Had a fantastic week—lost even more weight, and we were able to resist chips and salsa at our weekly "staff meetings" at La Cazuela, our Mexican restaurant of choice. The Smug Factor was high, and climbing.

Could not cover those ninety miles fast enough the next week. We were rapidly developing twin monkeys on our respective backs, which were becoming thinner by the day (the backs, not the monkeys): We *had to have* the needles, man. This time, the good doctor told us, he would be putting little balls in a bunch of spots on our ears—and leaving them there. It would be two weeks before we were to return. This registered with a sharp intake of breath from us. Two weeks? No way. We couldn't go two weeks without the needles, Doc. But he assured us we would be fine—better than fine. All we had to do when we felt the allure of chocolate or cheese or chimichangas was to rub on the little balls in our ears, which would stimulate the key pressure points, rendering the foodstuffs powerless over us. Ahhhh! The little balls—give them to us *now!* And so he did, and even though a couple of the needles poked out some true wincing and grimacing and a couple of borderline yowls, even so, the little balls were so worth it. They were tiny, tiny and *gold*, and they actually looked like some exotic ear jewelry thing. What a delicious secret we had—little-bitty, mysterious, but beautiful golden orbs shimmering about our ears, and only *we* knew their true power. We were practically drunk with Smug.

By the end of the two weeks, we had lost even more weight, and not surprisingly, we had worked so furiously on the balls that several of them, we feared, were permanently embedded in our flesh. Believing as we do that More Is More and therefore *better*, we thought that if a little stimulation to the pressure points would stave off hunger, then a lot would probably put us off our feed for the rest of our lives. So we were going for it, I'm saying. The nurses could not even conceal their green hides as they wrote down our dwindling weights on our charts, nor could we mask our truly unbearable level of smugness. We were the world's leading producers—and exporters—of Smug by this time. If you were sensing a peculiar lack of Smug in your ownself, and perhaps observing a similar loss in those around you, it was *our* fault. We had sucked up all the available supply in the universe and were hogging it for ourselves alone—without a trace of remorse, I might add.

The next time, the doc brought some much bigger guns to

the party, and even the thought of more lost poundage could not completely assuage our fears. There had been a couple of needles the time before—notably the ones in the big toes and between the eyes—that had produced at least a low level of levitation, but we'd managed to block the memory during the next fourteen days as the pounds fell away, naturally. This time, though, Tammy Donna was so afraid, she believed she'd have to have a turn on the table. Being nothing if not the very *soul* of solicitous, I hopped down and took her place on the opposing chairs. Well, we had to move my leg-propping chair so far away for me to achieve any sort of stretched-out position, the doctor couldn't get the door open, so that started us howling, which didn't make him any too happy.

We think, however, that the language barrier was more of a problem than anything: Our Chinese is not all it should be, even after twenty-some-odd years with Lance Romance, our beloved consort, who is, if you don't know, an actual Chinese person (even though on occasion he is mistaken for a Native American, but only by genuine idiots). We were convinced that if only our good doctor could fully *understand* us, he would then fully appreciate just how incredibly *funny* we actually were. It was, however, not to be. And this week, we were to get even bigger balls in our ears. And if there's anything we as Sweet Potato Queens really don't need, it's bigger balls, but that doesn't hamper our desire for them one whit. (Once again, that More Is More theory rears its head.)

So we were pretty taken with the prospect, and all was well

until I craned my neck around to where I could see what the doc was doing to Tammy Donna up there on my rightful table, and what I saw—well, it gave me pause, is all. All the beautiful tiny, golden balls from the previous visit were gone, pried out of their burrows by the good doctor, and had been replaced by significantly larger and very *black* balls. It looked like Tammy Donna had run through a patch of tall grass and come out with a whole family of ticks in her ears. I excused myself in a sudden manner, indicating an urge of an emergency nature, which allowed me to flee down the hall to the restroom, where I stuffed paper towels in my mouth to muffle the hee-hawing. But nothing could staunch the tears of mirth that flowed copiously down my face, neck, and bosom. My makeup was gone and my shirt was drenched by the time I made my way back to my position on the opposing chairs. Meanwhile, Tammy Donna was in a state of blissful meditation, contemplating her own impending state of thinness and utterly oblivious to the appearance of her little ears.

I silently endured my own session, including the application of my own personal set of ear ticks, and just waited. I knew sooner or later Tammy Donna would emerge from her contemplative state and be curious about what was going on down there on the chairs, and I was fairly squirming with anticipation. It was worth the wait. Nothing can describe the horror that was pouring off every syllable of whatever the words were that she uttered upon first sighting the black globules infesting my ears. The shriek that followed told me it had just dawned on her that her own personal ears looked a whole lot like mine. And the laughing that ensued, well, let me tell you it was like this: One of my very favorite ex-husband's favorite pastimes was embarrassing me, and one of his favorite ways of doing that was when we were in a crowded movie theater, preferably behind a semi-small child who would be incapable of ignoring him. The ex-husband would lean over and whisper to me that he possessed an uncanny ability to cast farts—a twisted sort of ventriloquism, if you will—and that he was presently going to pass a bit of noisy wind his ownself, but he was, with his great skill and sphincter dexterity, going to make it sound as if it came from a guy he had randomly selected, three or four rows down and to the right, whereupon he would just let fly with a veritable seat-ripper, which of course did not seem to come from anywhere else on earth than him, and the semi-small child would nudge his mama and start to comment and she would shush him and tell him to watch the movie and he would settle back down. So then, nothing would do but that the ex-husband had to come up with an even more impressive display of this warped "talent," and he would gesture, like a pool player calling his shots—"Redheaded guy, plaid shirt, two rows down, by the wall"—indicating the poor soul he intended to implicate in the next crime, and the sound he would emit could not be ignored by anyone short of Helen Keller. This would prove to be too much for the semi-small child, who, first glancing at his mama to be sure he was undetected, would slowly turn around and exchange a completely deadpan expression with the ex-husband, whereupon I would positively *erupt* into absolutely the most deliciously violent laughter ever experienced or heard by human beings. And of course, to this day, the semi-small child thinks it was *me*—the thought of which induces a like laughter in the ex-husband.

Well, that's how Tammy and I spent the next two weeks. Every time we caught a glimpse of each other's ears, we would blow Diet Pepsi out our respective noses and indulge in huge waves of belly laughs and guffaws of a most unladylike nature. There's no more immutable bonding experience that two people can share than making complete assholes of themselves together, in public. The really hilarious thing was here we were with four ears between us prominently infested with what appeared to be more ticks than the nastiest ole yard dog that ever lived—and nobody ever said a word. Not one. And neither did we. Oh, we'd see folks looking, all right; they couldn't help but look at 'em, in a kinda train wreck sort of way, but *nobody* ever said, "Hey, what the hell is that in y'all's *ears?*" Which, of course, made it even funnier to us.

The big balls definitely produced an accelerated level of weight loss, but as the next appointment time rolled around, we started remembering that the application had hurt ferociously in spots, and we were working up a fairly morbid fear of what the doc would do for an encore. When one of us had a conflict that meant rescheduling our appointment, we shared a big sigh of relief. After that, there was "always something" that would prevent a day trip to the needle doc. By and by, we quit even pretending we were going back. We were scared fat, but we didn't care. (Nobody knew about it, anyway—until now.) All that is to say we would—and have—done *anything* to lose weight, except, of course, the obvious one: changing our eating habits. Ha-ha-ha-ha—fat chance! Oh! *Ha-ha-ha-ha!* Get it? *Fat* chance.

So the knowledge that free-roaming, out there on this earth, right alongside our very selves, something exists that can make us *get skinny* by simply entering our personal spheres—well, like I said, it's the absolute Holy Grail, and for us, it wears pants. (So I can't really speak for you, but what I personally am looking for is not actually what you would normally define as "love" but rather a really good, amphetamine- and ephedrine-free, street-legal, and readily available appetite suppressant, and plenty of it.)

Yes, it wears pants, and we do so love it when it's tall, dark, and handsome, don't we? We also love it when it's gainfully employed and doesn't live with its mother. When you first meet Mr. Right—or at least Mr. Right Now—it's like magic. That is so trite but true. You look into each other's eyes (he's not looking over your shoulder at the blonde at the bar), your hands brush (he's not wearing a ring—neither wedding nor pinkie), you look down shyly (he's wearing good shoes and socks that are neither white nor nylon), your eyes meet again (he's still not noticing the blonde), you talk (he listens), he talks (somehow gracefully revealing his long-term, steady employment, his willingness and ability to compromise, and the fact that he recently built a small aircraft out of paper clips and gum and he invented the cat), perhaps you dance (he knows how to lead and he doesn't count under his breath), he pays the check (he *always* pays the check), he asks for your number (he puts it in the pocket of his pants, which are not too short, too long, too tight, or too high-waisted), you reluctantly part company for the evening after the perfect kiss (different for us all), and you close the door and realize *you're not hungry* (that's the "magic" part).

You're home, you're alone, it's late, there are tons of great black-and-white movies on television (even better, if you're lucky, there are *Law & Order* reruns out the ying-yang), there is some form of chocolate in the house, there is certainly popcorn if not actual Fritos, there is ice cream, there is cold pizza—you could, and normally *would*, pile up in the bed, blissfully alone with your raft of snack foods and Pepsi (diet, of course) and indulge in a healthy round of vacant mouth-breathing until the wee, wee hours, and . . . you . . . are . . . not . . . hungry. You get in bed and dutifully turn on the TV anyway, but not only are you not hungry, you can't properly focus on the mindless crap on the set before you. You're thinking—about *him*. You're remembering every single thing about him—what he said, what he didn't say, what he wore, how he smelled, his eyes, his smile, the way he moved, and, most important, that he has your phone number and promised to use it.

You scarcely sleep all night—you are too busy creating your fantasy life with him, and everybody knows that making up an entire future with another person you've known for only about six hours total is an incredible calorie-burner. It is easily the best exercise ever invented—way better than aerobics, weight lifting, Pilates, yoga, and any combination thereof. Why don't they ever tell you that on TV? That Denise Austin should quit prancing around every single morning of the world in her little leotard (with *no* tights, if you please), exhorting us all to mimic her every vigorous move—even during numerous commercial breaks—when you *know* she knows the Truth. I know she's got to support herself, and there are people paying her very well to make these false claims for exercise on national television every day. But can you imagine how much more she could make by bravely telling the Truth? Any woman who looks that good, under studio lights or in broad daylight—without tights—has clearly been up every night for the last ten or so years making up relationships with random and completely unsuspecting guys. I would pay large to hear her tell it all. I would buy any product that sponsored her—we all would.

You roll out of bed in the morning—you don't even feel tired—and you're still *not hungry*. You're so completely not hungry, you can pass up breakfast—even if somebody else has cooked it and it includes *bacon*. (This is the true love litmus for me—the ability to refuse bacon. In my normal state, I am completely powerless over bacon and my life is unmanageable because of it. The only piece of bacon I can control—sometimes—is the first one. One bite and I'm lost—a bacon-bender ensues and no pig is safe. If I am turning down already-cooked bacon that is set, sizzling, before me, I have clearly, as they say, Got It Bad.) Then you shower, imagining that, after a long night of fasting and full-fledged fantasy living, you're already feeling a new slimness, particularly in your hips and thighs. You dress, not failing to imagine that your slacks already zip up with greater ease. Ah yes, nothing facilitates an improvement in the zipping up quite as much as the urgent desire to zip *down*.

You go through your day in a blissful fog—you accomplish exactly nothing at work on account of it is very difficult to produce anything in this life when you are too busy living an imaginary life in a parallel universe where you and this guy are off into happily-ever-aftering—but, on the bright side, you're *still* not hungry. This is how it goes if you are like me and love to imagine that everything will turn out fine. I mean, what if it *did* for a change? It could happen, right? The not-hungry part is a by-product of the combination of the two or three really nice things that actually did happen in real life coupled with my hyperactive imagination, which visualizes this modest amount of happiness multiplying itself exponentially into several lifetimes of bliss—tempered with years of painful past experience that is screaming "Ha!" It's as if I've encountered a beautiful shoe, one of the best-looking shoes I've ever seen in my whole life, and as I gingerly pick it up and tentatively try to slip my foot into it—wonder of wonders! It fits and I can't believe my good fortune and then I realize—I've only got half the set here. So then I'm looking and waiting for the Other Shoe, not so much to *drop*, I wouldn't say—that would be a bit of a mercy, after all, wouldn't it? I can't recall ever having one just "drop."

No, it's usually more of a poke in the eye with the stiletto or a sharp rap between the eyes—even a forceful blow to the sensitive temple area—with a big ole chunky platform job.

I had a brief but memorable encounter with an initially lovely man once. All was so wonderful that I actually marveled aloud and commented that I was "waiting for the other shoe." And he said what I still consider to be one of the most romantic things ever said to me (even though it was a complete and total lie, as I was to find out within days). He took my hands and looked into my eyes and said, "I only have one shoe." And it just took my breath away. Okay, so he didn't have another *shoe*— what he had was more of a hip-wader filled with concrete—but it was still a nice thing to say, don't you think?

But anyway, when I'm moon-pied over a new guy, it's the threat of the Other Shoe that stomps out my appetite.

One of the Queens—it's that Tammy again, I swear—is just the opposite. She never thinks *anything* will work out. She suffers from pre-rejection at the moment of introduction, and while she, too, automatically projects an imaginary future life onto the screen of her mind, it's always a disaster that cannot wait to happen. She has gone through dozens of mental marriages—most of them ending badly—all in the time that occupies a mere weekend for most of us and, I might add, without the participation or in most cases even the knowledge of the other person. It's gotten to where, when she's relating the latest drama with the guy du jour, I have to ask her if this is something that *reeeally* happened—like where other people could see and hear it—or if it's another instance of her talking to the little man on her hand (you know, where you close your hand and paint a face on the side of it and wiggle your thumb up and down to make the mouth?).

Well, whenever she's off on a tangent and I am highly suspicious that she's making it up, all I have to do to flush her out is make my own little hand-man and talk in this high-pitched voice like Mr. Bill: "O-o-o-o-h, no-o-o-o! Tammy! Please don't cast me into outer darkness—we only just met. I haven't had time to need killin' yet. Don't throw me in the wood chipper, please—o-o-o-oh, no-o-o-o!" And she gets this sheepish look on her face and I know she's doing what she likes to call "reading between the lines" and I like to call "making shit up outta thin air." Tammy doesn't have imaginary friends—she has imaginary ex-husbands.

# 11

## Mucho Mojo

S o you've enhanced your lips and found new hair and waxed your hoo-hoo and emptied your child's college fund for a new face. Yet you still feel the need for a little something else to ensure your success at attracting and meeting men. How, you ask, to assure that you are *the* most irresistibly attractive woman on the premises? Excellent question. And so we sought counsel from none other than Chesley Pearman, world-renowned Mojo Expert. Our own Tammy Carol was going to France for an  extended stay and we wanted to be certain that she would have, shall we say, a really good time. Chesley sent us

## Mucho Mojo

the Most Powerful Juju Known—yes, I'm talking about the Otis Mojo, "guaranteed to make all mens 'be lovin' you too long." Chesley is King of Mojos, so he should know.

He says if you get a photograph of Otis Redding—preferably a black-and-white of him kneeling, in a complete state of frenzy with a microphone, but any Otis photo will work—and fold it up tiny, then slip it into the pocket or shoe of the man you desire, he will come running within twenty-four hours. You can also burn the Mojo and sprinkle the ashes in his food or drink, and it will work just as well. But you need to be careful when and where you use it. In a confined area, it could cause the complete breakdown of the moral fiber of every man in the place, according to Mojo King Chesley, and it could cause the total destruction of wooden-frame structures. He cautioned Tammy Carol about using the Otis Mojo abroad, warning that she could wake up and find herself the Queen of Some Foreign Country that doesn't even pick up Memphis radio. Consider yourself forewarned as well.

This folded-paper hoo-do reminds me of this elaborate process my daddy would go through to demonstrate a surefire method of determining whether or not a bill of any denomination was counterfeit. He would ask his victim for a bill, any bill, which the ninny would provide. Daddy would then go through an intricate and seemingly endless folding process on the bill, ending up with a tiny opening through which all that could be seen was one eyeball of whatever dead president was in residence. "There, you see?" Daddy would exclaim. *"This* one is genuine." And the ninny would say, "How can you tell?" To which Daddy would reply, completely deadpan, "If you fold it like this and you look through that little window and you see his asshole instead of his eyeball, you know it's counterfeit." Feel free to astonish your friends with this trick.

## PART IV

# Training and the Trainers

# 12

## Git Along, Little Donkey

My friend Candace Moody calls herself the luckiest woman, having been married to her precious darlin' husband, who is also a genuine massage therapist, for over twenty-five years. Her only problem is fending off all the women who want to steal him. I was tempted to try to get him for my very own self, but then I found the Cutest Boy in the World and found myself in the same boat of having the guy who's so perfect that everybody wants him. Candace suggested we have a Husband Summer Camp. I like her idea, but I don't think we ought to restrict it to the married. I think it should be an equal-opportunity training camp for all men interested in having relations, carnal or otherwise, with women. It would also be possible for women to have their men committed against their will and held until properly educated.

As it happens, I was at the Neshoba County Fair with my friend Allen Payne, and while we were touring the 4-H Building, we picked up some very informative flyers about the National Mule Association. We're joining, of course—not because we own mules or even know very much about actual mule animals but because we know a whole lot about being *muley,* and we figure that qualifies us for lifetime membership. (If you happen to be either a Yankee or from another planet where they don't have mules, you may not understand this reference. Mules are noted for, among other things, sitting down, frowning, in the middle of the road with their ears laid back, refusing to budge or do anything else.) My sister, Judy (as in Judy Conner, author of *Southern Fried Divorce,* which you should read ASAP—you can get your own copy at sweetpotatoqueens.com), is probably some kind of world champion of Muley, and I learned a lot from her growing up. Allen, on the other hand, is an only child, so he had to learn it on his own, but his partner, Jeffrey Gross, assures me that Allen is qualified to give Muley lessons, in case anybody in the New York City area feels he or she has been a bit too flexible and compliant lately.

But anyway, amid all the mule literature we snagged, I found a big section on donkeys—that is, the training of donkeys. It struck me as a good plan for our Man Training Camp as well. I'm going to give you some of the high points from "Your Young Donkey—An Owner's Manual," published in *The Brayer*, the members' magazine of the American Donkey and Mule Society (see www.lovelongears.com—I swear). Whenever I refer to the "donkey," you'll know to change it in your mind to "man."

- You should know that, as a conscientious donkey owner, you will be walking a fine line between having a donkey as a friend and partner or one who is obnoxious and spoiled.

- Always remember that your donkey is a donkey and as such, its behavior will be that of a donkey. For instance, donkeys play rough with one another. One of their favorite "games" is "tag"—where one donkey will race up to another one with its mouth open, bite the second donkey, whirl around and kick at it, and then race off, bucking and kicking. And this is perfectly acceptable behavior between donkeys; however, it is not generally acceptable between donkeys and people. You need to be very clear up front with your donkey that you are *not a toy.*

- You shouldn't ever slap at your donkey when it's in a nipping or biting phase. Young donkeys want to put their mouths on any and every thing. You should just gently push his head away and firmly say "no." Slapping at them makes them aggressive. If the behavior persists after several gentle "no's," simply put the donkey up and walk away from him.

- Donkeys are like young children and it sometimes takes a while for them to learn good behavior. [This next part is very, very important.] *There is absolutely no point in picking a fight with your donkey.* [It's apparently the equivalent of teaching a pig to sing—wastes your time and annoys the pig.]

- Keep your lessons short and sweet. Donkeys are suspicious of things they aren't familiar with, and it may take many lessons in small doses in order to desensitize them. By all means, use a "butt rope"—literally, a rope tied around their butt—as a "come along" to assist you. [This would be especially helpful in training your donkey to go into new and unfamiliar territory, such as jewelry stores.] Sometimes it helps also to give them a little feed [beer and a sammich] in the new and unfamiliar territory, just to let them see that they are safe and that nothing will "get them" in the new and unfamiliar territory. Donkeys apparently believe that many donkey-eating booger-bears hide in such places.

- Teaching your donkey to stand while tied to a fence or something is a very important part of its training. *Never tie your donkey to anything that will move;* otherwise, what's the point of tying it?

## Git Along, Little Donkey

- The Donkey Trainer summed up by telling us: Your friendship with your donkey can be one of the most rewarding and loving relationships of your life. Donkeys are quite simply some of the most wonderful folks around. Good luck with yours.

I should think those points would be in our *Basic* Training Class. For more advanced students, we would move into specialized areas of particular interest to us. For instance, we would want to teach the man to give a good massage. One of the most important parts of this lesson would be the Difference Between Two Minutes of Back Massage and Foreplay. (We'll have to get Tammy to take this class.) We would also want to offer a class on female anatomy and include a frank and graphic description of the aforementioned foreplay—which, by the way, should *not* include anything that resembles a woodpecker after a pine beetle, starting a siphon, or stuffing banknotes up a chimney.

We would also teach them to cook at least one elegant and romantic meal, and include instruction on purchasing flowers and setting the table—as well as clearing the table and loading the dishwasher.

There would be a workshop where the trainees are required to make a list of all the reasons they love their wives/partners. They would be instructed to refer to this list frequently, both mentally and verbally, and occasionally to commit it to writing and submit it to their wives/partners.

Gift Giving 101 would include safe generic shopping techniques for the unattached as well as Advanced Gift-Specific Shopping for those currently in relationships and Emergency Suck-Up Gift Shopping for those who have been committed to the camp involuntarily. Participants would learn that while it is totally acceptable, even desirable, to buy a diamond that is just *too big*, the same cannot be said for lingerie, and if you buy something that is too small, it's bad whether it's diamonds or lingerie, hence the safest gift is a big-ass diamond-something. This should be simple enough for all participants to grasp.

Upon graduation, each candidate would be issued an Official Sweet Potato Queens' Oh Shit Kit™, which includes a form for him to complete, listing all-important gift-giving dates. (We thought about making this a wallet card but decided it needs to be at least poster-size to get his attention. It should be mounted someplace he frequents regularly, like on the door of the fridge that houses his beer perhaps, or on the wall of his workshop, or under the hood of his car, or on the ceiling above the couch where he watches football.) Additional instructions direct him to begin the gift-shopping procedures at least one week prior to the date of the required gift giving, also known as the drop-dead date. Wallet cards on which he can record the names and numbers of an excellent florist and a quality jeweler also contain pre-printed Suck-Up Phrases, which he may use in written form or verbally in accompaniment with the proffered flowers and sparklies. A genuine Official SPQ tiara is included in case he forgets to use the Oh Shit Kit™ in a timely fashion and all the stores are closed. He can present the crown, with the appropriate, total suck-up (included) wording on the gift card, and then take her out for a fancy dinner. Finally, a suitable length of sturdy rope is included with which he can hang himself if he fails to do any of the above. (You can order an Oh Shit Kit™ for your Spud Stud™ right now at sweetpotatoqueens.com.)

# 13

## Surviving the Wang Wars

Alas and alack, love does occasionally derail, and when it does, it usually wipes out entire neighborhoods, releases a massive cloud of terminally toxic gas, and the cleanup can take years. And while it may be true that it is not *always* their fault when things go awry, it is no less true that we certainly *believe* that it's always their fault and we want 100 percent of all the blame to be laid not so much at their feet but rather on top of their bodies, making it impossible for them to breathe and continue living in any real sense of the word. What would really make us just oh so happy is to be allowed to murder them ten different times in ten different ways and then finally feed the remains to the wood chipper. But hardly anybody ever really gets to do that. And so, barring that ultimate satisfaction, a number of Queens have demonstrated characteristic Queenly Resourcefulness in their dealings with errant mates in ways that are not likely to land the perpetrator in the slammer, and that's a Good Thing. I share them with you as food for thought—fodder for your consideration as alternative strategies should you find yourself currently in possession of a man who is just beggin' to be killed.

Once upon a time, my friend Lori was dating the conductor on the train she took to work each day. But soon she learned he was not just a cute conductor guy but also a low-down, two-timing, not-even-that-cute piece of shit. So the next day, when he came through the car to punch everybody's tickets, she just smiled up at him, sweet as you please, and handed him a replica of a genuine ticket that she had made her ownself at home, and instead of having the destination, it said, "Fuck you, Bob!" It really improved for her what would have otherwise been a long and boring commute.

Picture it: Oklahoma City, in the nineties. Queen Stormie was possessed of what she thought was a very fine fiancé— a well-respected physician. He appeared to be "perfect"— perfect practice, perfect house and grounds. It seemed as if every little ole thing about this guy was perfect, right down to his carefully selected and maintained Armani suits and Porsche Boxter. And you know what they say about stuff that seems too good to be true—yep, there's gonna be a turd in the chimney corner *somewhere* that will ultimately stink up the world as you know it.

And naturally, Dr. Perfect was no exception. He was, in fact, the walking, talking illustration of the principle. Actually, from Stormie's description of him, at first he sounded like a classic Fuddy-Dud Spud to me, but he was a hybrid—a combo of Fuddy-Dud and Blood Spud. It turned out he saw himself as a Healer of Women and had multiple, simultaneous fiancées scattered all over town. When Stormie first got wind of this possibility, she and her band of angels investigated and found irrefutable EOW (evidence of other women), so they sprang into action without a moment's hesitation. They had to make a split-second decision whether to approach this situation from the Fuddy-Dud or the Blood Spud angle. As I've said so often before and I'll continue to say, you really and truly just can*not* kill them, it will only make more trouble for yourself, and I'm happy to report that Stormie and her pals remembered that.

They jumped into their speedy roadsters and dashed to the closest convenience store and purchased twelve cans of "whomp" biscuits (you know, the kind in a can that you whomp on the counter to open—I know that the labels say "press on the seam with a spoon," but nobody has ever done that ever in the history of the world and canned biscuits). This amounted to two cans per girl. For the purpose at hand, there is no need to buy the brand name; generic whomps will do just fine.

The girls, loaded to the eyeteeth with cheap whomp biscuits, made their way to his big-ass, fancy house in his big-ass, fancy neighborhood, and even though there was nobody around for blocks and it was pitch-black, they chose to utilize the time-honored crawl-on-your-belly-like-a-reptile method of approaching the house—primarily because it amused them to do so, and I have to admit, it does add a certain something to the event. So they slithered, while giggling uncontrollably, all the way through the yard, hiding behind trees when the opportunity presented itself and acting like Navy SEALS on a secret mission. Finally they reached lobbing distance of the house. After the traditional count of three, the air was thick (not to mention doughy) with flying whomps. We can easily imagine the satisfying *shhhpoick* sound they must have made as they reached their target—the bricked front of the big-ass house. And you may not be aware—but for future reference you certainly need to be—that whomp dough just loves brick, and apparently the feeling is mutual, because once the two are brought together, it's just dang near impossible to separate them. Can't we imagine the little Fuddy-Dud and his frenzied scrubbing? Yes, yes, we can.

I wonder if this hint, of how to get back at an ex, has ever appeared in Heloise's books? She really should consider a book of helpful revenge hints like this. Then she could follow up with a list of antidotes for the victims. For instance, Heloise would no doubt suggest that the Fuddy-Dud try scrubbing those whomps off his bricks with nylon net.

If the idea of modestly defacing the property of others gives you a little twitch, you'll want to contemplate the next suggestion as well. Bumper stickers can be very difficult to remove, especially when one doesn't notice it for a month or so. I cannot divulge the slightest hint of the identity of the guilty party, but it seems that her husband's best friend had a wife who was simply intolerable to everyone, the best friend (her husband) included. And so when our friend saw a particular bumper sticker, the unblissful couple immediately came to mind and she purchased it on the spot. It read YOUR WIFE'S A BITCH . . . AND THEN YOU DIE. Ha-ha-ha-ha—so much funnier than the old "Life's a bitch," don't you think? When our friend just happened to see the couple's car parked in an accessible spot, well, she simply could not be expected to resist slapping it on the bumper, and indeed she did not—resist, that is. And she was very nearly caught by some of the Baptists as they came out of the church to the parking lot where the car was. Thank goodness she didn't *dance* her way back to her own car!

My very good friend Queen Aubergine had this one husband for a 'coon's age—nearly thirty years—and over the course of those years, she performed innumerable feats to demonstrate her love and devotion to him. But one of the sweetest things she ever did sadly turned out a year later to be his own personal petard upon which she hoisted him. Ahhh, karma—it's a beautiful thing.

Here's what happened. Her PITA (term of endearment for "pain in the ass") had racks of suits and fine clothes that he wore just once a year, when his industry had their annual convention. He waged a constant losing battle with his bulges, and every single year, right before convention time, the same sad scene would play out at their house: He would try on his suits and they would all be too tight, and he would pitch a fit, and then be depressed over his most recent "growth spurt." I have to admit, I can relate. But anyway, one year, Aubergine had a brilliant and loving idea. She took all his clothes to the tailor and had them all let out—*before* he ever tried them on. Oh, was he ever a happy boy when he was able to just slide right into them. He was just *so* pleased with himself for not gaining weight that year—and bless her heart, she never told him what she had done. That was just an act of pure love, if you ask me, and Lord, how I wish somebody would do it for me.

So how does he repay her for thirty years of selfless devotion? We discovered that he'd been cheating on her at this same convention each and every year for their whole married life. Our Aubergine, though, she kept her head—did she ever. Convention time rolled around again, and again she secretly had his clothes altered, and again he tried them on successfully and congratulated himself on yet another year without gaining weight. A few days before his departure, however, while he was no doubt distracted with thoughts of his svelte self with the convention ho, our Aubergine snuck out with his clothes again and had them all *taken in*. Buttons were moved over at least two inches; inseams were shortened by a few as well. In addition, ties were besmirched with whipped cream, shirt cuffs were frayed, a few buttons went missing, and his favorite sweater developed a mothy-looking hole at the neckline. And then, without even a telltale smirk on her beautiful, formerly trusting face, she packed him all up and sent him off to his beloved convention. And then, of course, she divorced him. Gosh, I'm such a sucker for a happy ending.

Men might want to be on especially good behavior if they are involved with Women Who Sew. This group is quiet but merciless. Witness this tale of a well-timed stitch. The wise and wonderful Suki Buttons was vewy, vewy angwy with her first hubby. Now, up until that very day, butter had never melted in Suki's mouth, so cool and serene was her normal temperament, but as we see, cool and serene are not synonymous with doormat. He pissed her off; he would pay—it's a simple law of nature. So, with very small and precise stitches, she sealed the fly on his boxers and put them back in the drawer. The next day, at his industrial roofing job, he nearly turned the Port-A-John over trying to, ah, get hold of himself, as it were, and woe was him, he could not find a way in. He fished around wildly, looking for the fly that had never before failed to be there since his first pair of training pants, but it was there no more. He finally decided he must have somehow put his panties on backward, but by the time he fully realized that he couldn't get in by the usual route and reviewed alternative options, his time had run out—and so had everything else. Don't you just know his burly coworkers were understanding and kind to him about the whole thing? Guys are so sweet like that.

# Surviving the Wang Wars

At the beginning of this book, I opined that relationship stuff is prolly pretty much the same for us all, straight or gay, but I set out to explore that concept a bit just to confirm my good insight. And of course, I was right, and this did not surprise me. I began my research on our message board, and the Marquis informed me that, while he himself was not at all the vengeful type, he had picked up a few pointers from his good friend Bruce. Bruce has a black belt in revenge and he isn't afraid to use it. Bruce had once been "married to" (meaning at that time, in gay circles, "living with and frequently wearing matching outfits," according to our Marquis) a guy whose name has long since been deliberately forgotten, given the level of acrimony present at their breakup. What's-His-Name kept the house *and* the new car. Some time later, Bruce mentioned to one of their neighbors (Bruce kept the friends) that he was thinking of buying the same kind of car for himself, and the neighbor said, "Omigod, don't do that. What's-His-Name has just had a *time* with that car. It leaks oil by the bucket, and no matter how many times he takes it in, the mechanic cannot figure out why." Mmmmm-hmmmm, Bruce was so grateful for that warning, or so he told the neighbor. In truth, Bruce knew exactly why that car was "leaking" oil: He had been going over to What's-His-Name's house on a regular basis and dribbling oil on the pavement under the car!

My dear friend and sometimes workout buddy James had been regaling me for weeks with tales of this delicious new lawyer-boyfriend he was considering elevating to fiancé status. Well, before that could happen, they went on a date and, as it happened, a lot of Perry Mason's other buddies were out that night and he just totally ignored sweet baby James all night long. They were at a gay bar, so it was not a question of being "out"— it was just ass-monkey behavior at its worst (apparently being straight is not a requirement for being an ass-monkey). But did our James sit and nurse his hurt feelings over this? Not a chance. He took a big dose of I'll-teach-you-to-fuck-with-*me* elixir and he felt better fast, fast, fast! Bright and early the next morning, James called his favorite florist (Petal Pushers, no doubt— they're everybody's favorite florist), and he sent ole Perry Mason the biggest, flashiest, *gayest* bouquet of flowers ever seen outside of Munchkinland with a handwritten note (and no envelope) that read, "Had a fabulous time last night—next time *I'll* be the girl! See you in the chat room this afternoon, precious!" and sent it to Perry's law office. That little bit of revenge is so sweet it makes my teeth hurt.

A true Tammy from Texas wrote to report that her very own Tater Tot, now grown, had demonstrated to her mama's utter satisfaction that she had, in fact, been raised right, and not as anybody's fool, either. The precious child was only twenty-four and she'd been dating this tall, dark, and studly thang for several years. They'd talked of marriage after college—although the absence of any *ring* from him was conspicuous. The baby girl had helped him get into a really good school, helped him study, helped support him, and all that crap, because they were in loooove, don'tcha know. And then, after a spring break trip to Cozumel—for which she naturally paid the lion's share—he got to studying a little too late, a little too often. And so the raised-right nonfoolish child eased around and caught the bastard "in flagrante poontang," as they say.

She did not even allow him to know that she knew—no, ma'am, she did not. She took herself on back home and had a good cry and then, by and by, the storm passed and she recollected that there was a whole suitcase full of his personal clothing in the back of her very own car, which she had, of course, personally laundered, folded, and repacked after their trip. Well, that thought just perked her up no end, and she skipped out to the curb and retrieved the bag (I imagine she was humming softly under her breath). She then grabbed a pair of cheerful yellow rubber gloves and toted the suitcase to the back fence, where there grew and prospered an absolute *wealth* of vibrant poison ivy vines. Emptying the suitcase on the ground and donning the gloves (by now she was clearly *singing*, possibly an aria), she lovingly plucked up each and every garment and rubbed it vigorously in the poison ivy, devoting extra time and effort to items with *crotches*. She thoughtfully refolded and packed all the items, making sure to eliminate any wrinkles, so that they would all be ready for him to wear when she dropped them off at his door—he was used to the home-delivery system. Then she moved on, without giving him so much as another thought.

Oh! I don't mind telling you, I got a little misty as I read this—to live long enough to see your own child rubbing poison ivy in the crotch of some jackass's underpants. Well, it's just every mother's dream. We should all be so blessed.

One of my very favorite Queens (who shall remain nameless in case by now Santa has actually brought her her very own wood chipper) once lost a both a kidney and a husband on the very same day—although she didn't consider either one a "loss." It seems their precious daughter needed a kidney. Luckily, she and her husband were excellent matches. His kidney was ever so slightly better than her own, though, so the doctors deemed it best to use it, and soon—within the next two weeks. When she called him at work to let him know what the doctors had said, he said she'd have to hold on a minute while he checked his work schedule.

By the time the sumbitch got back on the line, Queenie had lined up (1) the surgeon to remove her own kidney and place it lovingly in her daughter and (2) the lawyer to remove her sorry-ass husband from her life and place him not so lovingly at the curb.

Okay. Here's a dab of behavior modification you can try on him. What the hell—it can't hurt, right? I mean, he runs around like a spotted-ass ape right now—anything would be an improvement in my estimation. Okay, so when they're being butt-headed, we like to call them ass-hats. (I'm not certain of the derivation of that particular name, but to *me*, it seems like it must have something to do with him being so completely self-absorbed as to have his own head pretty far up his own ass—which from some vantage points might make it appear as if he has on an actual ass-hat, and thus, the name.) Now, as the Tammys will tell you, I am fairly superstitious—there are many jujus that can bring bad luck. Fifty-dollar bills, for instance. I will not touch one. They are bad luck. Ask any gambler. It is also extremely bad luck to put shoes on the bed. If you accidentally do this, you must quickly remove the shoes and kiss the bottoms of them—I don't care where they've been, you kiss 'em, and if it makes you gag, good, it'll help you remember next time to *not put your shoes on the bed!* And it is reeeally bad luck to put a hat on the bed.

So we wanted a way to communicate to the Man that we had noticed that he was behaving like an ass-hat and that it was going to bring him *very* bad luck if he didn't smarten his ass up pretty quick. We didn't have, or want, a hat that actually looks like a butt hanging around the house—because you *know* he'd want to wear it to cut the grass or something, and next thing you know, he'd forget and go to Wal-Mart in it. So we decided a Skunk Hat was just the thing. If he comes in and sees that there is a hat on the bed, he knows that is a Bad Thing, but if he further sees that it is a Skunk Hat and that it is on his side of the bed—well, let's just say, this bodes far worse for him than any ole black cat crossing his path ever could. He should infer from that omen that a genuine, real, live, spotted-ass ape would stand a better chance of getting some that night. If you've got an ass-hat at your house, visit our Web site (sweetpotatoqueens.com), where we have a full stock of Skunk Hat Training Devices. We think the Skunk Hat will turn quickly into a good-luck charm—he will evolve into a fully upright primate and you will feel amorous toward him once more. How lucky is that?

# 14

# You Can't Make Nothing but a Man out of Him

If we insist on being involved with men (and I for one have never found an acceptable long-term substitute), about the only thing we can realistically expect to manage is expectations—namely our own. It is best for all concerned if we can remember just who it is that we are involved with— a *man*—and downshift way, way down; I'd say just go on into four-wheel drive and stay there.

One of our favorite Wannabes just called, having forty fits over stuff her husband has done while home from work on vacation leave. Well, I could see the problem right there before she even got started on the details—if it's vacation leave, he should have to *leave.* Am I right? Why should he get to hang around the house and make more work for her? And boy, did he ever. He rearranged everything in all their kids' rooms—without talking to the kids first—and expected *her* to smooth things over with them once they came home. He "landscaped" the yard— meaning he went out and rented some equipment to play with and dug a bunch of holes in which nothing ever got planted, of course, because he ran out of time playing with the equipment. And so the holes remain and they're not getting any better look- ing with time. He offered to teach her to cook—*so she could finally learn*—and when she came back to the house after a rather abrupt leave-taking (no doubt to cool off enough so as to spare his life), he had reorganized *her* kitchen "so it made sense." It took her three hours to make dinner because she couldn't find anything. The kids were whining because they were hungry and their rooms were all screwed up. It took her another couple hours afterward to clean up the kitchen because she couldn't remember where the new location for everything was. *And then* he wanted to have sex! *With her!* We suggested that she deep- breathe and relax and go to a quiet, calm, orderly place in her mind—like maybe visualizing *his* garage and workshop and closet when she gets through reorganizing them "so they make sense." That certainly had the desired effect—instantaneously, too, I might add. I think she may have even been a little turned on by the prospect, so perhaps he got lucky that night after all.

# You Can't Make Nothing but a Man out of Him

———

One of our little Larva Queens (anyone under forty is larva) came by the other day in a swivet because she'd had a date with a new cute guy who said he would call and then—disbelieving gasp!—he didn't. You know, it's now, what, 2004? I swear, ever since telephones were invented, guys have been *not* using them when they're supposed to, and we have been bitching about it nonstop. Wouldn't you think they would have heard about it by now and straightened up? I mean, do we think there is a guy living somewhere in the civilized world today who is unaware that this makes women insane? That somehow he just hasn't gotten that word? I can't believe there is even one.

They *all* know better, and they act like ass-monkeys anyway. It's damn hard not to take it personally. But we just can't. They are guys, they always were guys, they're gonna always *be* guys, and there's nothing to be done about it. Except as I said, manage our own expectations. Or think of another way to look at the situation. I'm a big proponent of the There's Always Another Way of Looking at It school of thought.

Tammy Carol says, usually in a not particularly kind way, that she will personally see to it that those words are etched on my tombstone. I suppose it *is* annoying, when one is in the middle of a fit, to be told by your bosom buddy that perhaps there's another possible viewpoint in the universe. But I find that it's rarely helpful to agree with a distraught person that all is lost. A solution *does* exist somewhere, and it's best to begin the hunt for it sooner rather than later. Too much time is spent discussing what the problem is, when everybody and their grandmother already *knows* what the problem is. What remains to be seen— and the only thing of any value—is the solution.

Every female I know, myself included, has spent hours of perfectly good life agonizing over why some guy hasn't called. And every friend of those females has spent hours with her, in the same agony, rationalizing and thinking and interpreting every single detail of every single word ever said by the guy, and his facial expression at the time, and his body language, and the phase of the moon, and all we've managed to glean about him from every source available, from Google to old girlfriends. And all this conjecture could not be worth less if we just sat and made up shit about guys we'd never met or even laid eyes on before. It is a complete and utter waste of everybody's time. Yet we seem to be incapable of refraining from it. We could go to medical school—and come out with multiple specialties—in the cumulative time we have spent mooning around trying to figure out why some guy hasn't called.

In contrast, let's examine what happens if, for some unknown reason, they are expecting a call from *us* that never comes. I can tell you in one word. Nothing. No-thing. They do not think about it *at all*. They simply move on to more promising pastures. They do not call all their guy friends in the middle of the night to cry about it. They do not meet for lunch and then drinks and then dinner multiple times to discuss all the possible explanations for our lapse. They do not try to weasel information out of our friends, which they can then turn around and distort into something hopeful for themselves. They don't imagine that we are "commitment-phobes" or that we have just been "so hurt" by past relationships that we are paralyzed with fear. They don't worry that they said or did some terribly wrong thing that scared us off. They just assume that there are one of two possible explanations for the fact that we are not currently hanging off the end of their dicks: (1) We are simply not interested in them for some unknowable reason, or (2) we're gay. But none of that really matters to them. All that matters to them is that we're not hanging off the end of their dicks. So they immediately turn to the pressing matter at hand, and that would be finding one who *will*, and quick.

Frankly, I think it's time we take a page out of their book. The next time a guy you have a remote interest in fails to call you when he says he will, do not ponder the potential whys and wherefores of the situation. If at all possible, be so busy with your own wonderful life that you simply don't even notice that he hasn't called. It would be great if you could just be so involved having a Big Time with all the people in your life who do right that if in fact he *does* call at some point, it takes you a minute to remember who he is.

If he doesn't call, don't try to figure out acceptable excuses for the guy—and don't try to make yourself believe that he's going to call, either. Just assume that he's just not that into you—as unbelievable as that seems—and move on. Don't take it personally. After all, how many men are there out there in the world who *you* are not attracted to? Plenty. And that's not personal: We can't really control our feelings of attraction and the lack thereof. Either you are or you are not, and that's pretty much that. Have you ever tried to *get* attracted to some guy just because he looks so good on paper? Nice enough looking, good job, decent human, etc.—but he just doesn't have "it." You tell yourself that "it" might develop over time; after all, he's clearly not a hound from hell. You keep going out with him because you ought to—and you feel worse every date. Awful, isn't it? There's nothing worse and nothing more impossible than trying to manufacture "it." "It" is spontaneous combustion. This concept makes sense to us when we are not attracted to *them*. So when one of them is not attracted to us, we should not consider it the end of our world. Move on, hunny—just move on.

Most of the time, when a guy doesn't call, he thinks he's easing out gracefully and sparing our feelings. *Because that's how guys think.* If they try to call us a few times and we don't respond, they get the message and go on off somewhere else. They move quickly into acceptance and regrouping. I actually once had a guy do me the great service—and I mean that with all sincerity—of just telling me he wasn't that into me. In *The Sweet Potato Queens' Book of Love,* I told the tale of the guy from Pittsburgh. Yes, well, we made right good fun of him in that text, and in real life, too, but the truth is, even though it seemed insane at the time, since he'd been all over me every moment right up to the moment of the dumpage, I chose just to accept it for the fact it was and move on. I never shed one tear; never tried to win him back in any way. I just expressed mild surprise (huh?) and moved on. It was very freeing. And he and I are great friends to this very day.

Don't agonize over what could possibly be wrong with you that he doesn't want you—it really is not personal. For whatever reason, you don't have "it" for him and that's okay. And for God's sake, please do not write him any letters. I know, I know. You think—we all think—that they just need to *understand* this, that, and the other thing, and when they understand, everything will be different. It won't. He already understands everything he needs to—*he is not into you*—and every word you *do not say* to him on the subject will come back to help you, very soon. When you've recovered from the shock of not being the center of somebody's universe, all those words you *did not say* will be like love letters to yourself, because you will have something he cannot give you: your own personal dignity—remember that? And yes, while it's true that dignity will not keep you warm at night, it's just as true that the absence of it will chill your soul. I vote for the electric blanket and the dignity for a total warmth experience.

So in the absence of a call, don't devote any precious girlfriend time to the divination of the possible reasons for this gross lapse in manners and this inexplicable failure of his to avail himself of the company and attentions of the world's most amazing woman (you). Why would we want to spend any time at all thinking about somebody who is clearly not thinking about us? Our time is better utilized in scoping out the ones who are, and rewarding that good behavior. But if you just absolutely *must* have a satisfactory explanation for why he hasn't called, how about this: What if he was dead? He couldn't call then, now could he? We know that he wanted to—more than anything—but dead guys don't ever call, and even if they did, they don't have any money and you can't fuck 'em, so what's the point? You cannot date the dead—nobody can. It's not even an acquired taste, like stamp collectors or something—they are completely unsuitable, the ultimate sow's ear. So I'm telling you, if he doesn't call, assume he's dead. You and your girl-friends can be absolutely certain that he *intended* to call. You can even say you know for a fact that he was *dead* to call you (tee-hee). Perhaps he was even *trying* to call you (a) on his cell phone and he drove his Pinto smack into the ass end of a cattle truck, or (b) on his home phone, which was struck by lightning, or perhaps (c) from a roadside pay phone and he was the unfortu-nate victim of yet another senseless drive-by shooting.

That cute Laurie Roberts says sometimes she leaves a loop-hole in this and only has them seriously ill, as in "Hear from so-and-so?" "No, he's coughing up blood." That way, if he does call, he can recover, but it's easy enough to eliminate him if he doesn't. Perfect. You can kill him off however it suits you, and tsk-tsk over the tragic waste of life and sigh over the missed opportunity. But as they say, life is for the living, and you, Miss Livewire, must move on. And when someone asks you, "Whatever happened to old Hoochipap Whateverhisnamewas?" just look pensive and say, "Oh, didn't you hear? He died," and change the subject.

Now, suppose you then run into him, living and breathing,

out and about somewhere. Or what if, by and by, he ups and calls? Fine. Two plausible explanations: Miracle of Modern Medicine or, more likely, it's his identical twin, who nobody knew about before now—just like in the soaps. Growing up, back when television was invented, I remember Daddy coming home for lunch every day and him and Mama sitting down in the living room to watch *As the World Turns.* I never thought about it at the time, but what do you reckon she was doing to get him to do *that?* Now, there's some food for thought.

# 15

## There's Always Tater Love

Queen Susie wrote that she'd been enjoying a totally felicitous relationship with her new pig and that she was happier with this pig than she had ever been with any man so far in her life—although she admitted to being on the young side and hopeful for the future. It seems that she had the great good fortune of finding a pig that was just the right size and shape. (I myself had never considered there was much room for variation, figuring they all were pretty much, well, *pig*-shaped, but this was her story, so I let her tell it.) Susie's pig was very well-behaved: He never picked fights, nor was he contrary in any way; he never hurt her feelings, nor was he overly sensitive himself. He was always there when she called and happy to stay in his place when she didn't. They spent every night together, and he was ready to hit the road with her at a moment's notice—or less. Her pig was particularly entertaining on long car trips, thankfully not a chatterbox, and they were comfortable together in silence. He was an excellent listener, too. Both their energy level and desire for activity seemed well-matched. So often a party animal finds oneself paired with a slugabed—but not so with Suze and her pig. He would and could and did happily go for as long as she wanted.

I was somewhat taken aback when she said that she had never been so completely satisfied sexually before in her life. I had never met Susie before, and I was somewhat agog that this near-stranger felt comfortable not only confessing her sexual dalliances with a farm animal but raving so about them, so much so that I began to think the lowly pig had been woefully disregarded by us all for lo, these many years. Only then did I realize my mistake—Susie was referring not to the lower-case "pig" of my shocked imagination but rather to the upper-case acronym "P.I.G."—Plug-In Guy! "Oh!" I said, with no small amount of relief. She's talking about her vibrator!

You know, hardly a day goes by that somebody doesn't send me those "tater" jokes—you know, the common-taters, the speck-taters, etc. They were funny the first five hundred times, but I swear, the humor has worn off for me now. But here I go, anyway. I guess the vibrator—the vibra-tater!—could also be the agi-tater (he'll get you all worked up). He's definitely the imi-tater (make-believe man), and some versions could be called dick-taters, I suppose! *We* still like to call him "Bob" (battery-operated boyfriend), just because we never met a Bob, human or otherwise, we didn't purely love.

# 16

## Because You're Worth It

The phrase "because you're worth it" doesn't apply just to hair color and cosmetics, you know. Here's a mystery: A woman will all but spend her rent money on her clothes, her makeup, her coiffure, her Pilates classes, and, let us not forget, her *shoes*—because she is totally worth it and she knows it. She will go to tremendous trouble and expense taking good care of her physical self, and yet this very same woman will completely trash herself emotionally and spiritually in rotten relationships with men. Somebody explain that to me, please. I've said it before and I'll say it again: A Boyfriend

Who Sucks Is Not Better than No Boyfriend at All. A Boyfriend Who Sucks Is a Boyfriend Who Sucks!

If you're currently in an unhappy, destructive relationship with a man, try this little exercise: Whatever bad behavior the guy is manifesting—anything from drinking, lying, cheating, stealing, or using you for a punching bag to merely taking you for granted and being constantly critical or inattentive—write it all down, all the infractions, big and small. Then ask yourself, "Would I accept this kind of treatment from a female friend?"

My friend Martha from Tupelo was going with a guy who was—I am not lying or exaggerating—a practicing drug addict with no car or house or job. He never did anything he promised when he said he would. He brought drugs into her house, convinced her to drive him to buy drugs in her car, and he had four kids his wife left him with! Now, I promise, Martha is a smart, beautiful, charming, successful, desirable woman. And *that* is her boyfriend?! Whenever I would get in her face about it—which was every time I talked to her for six months—she would tell me how cute and funny and talented he *really* was and how everybody was just crazy about him. "Oh, yeah, like *who*, for instance? Is it those four kids he's 'supporting' in such fine style? Or all the people who have to pick up the slack for his sorry ass so he can pursue his chosen profession of pot smoking?"

Nothing got through to her. She just refused to see the truth. But one day I finally thought of comparing him to a girlfriend. She and I both know a woman in Tennessee who is, shall we say, long overdue for a stay at the Betty (the Betty Ford treatment place, you know). We'll just call her Shanequa, since to the best of my knowledge, we don't actually know anybody by that name. I said to her, "Martha, if your boyfriend is so fine just like he is, how come you don't hang out with Shanequa? I mean, she's drunk all the time, she hasn't worked in twenty years, and she's got some kids she doesn't take care of. If that's what you're looking for in a relationship, how come you're not best friends with Shanequa? You could get her to move to Tupelo, persuade your daddy to give her a job in the family business. Then you could take her to all those civic functions you're involved in—even get her to be your roommate! Shanequa is every bit as talented and cute as that boy you've been wagging around with you everywhere. And I know all your friends in town will agree." She was taken aback. I knew she would set herself on fire before she'd let the people she cares for and respects associate her with the slatternly Shanequa. For some reason—could it be the sheer *logic* of it all?—she heard that and finally understood. She dumped the guy the next week, thank God!

So if you're in a crappy relationship, and all your girlfriends are telling you it's crappy, and you're feeling crappy all the time but you still won't walk away from it, put it to the Girlfriend Test. If your girlfriend treated you the way this guy does, would you still be friends with her? If the answer is no, then get out of it. And, mercy, if the answer is yes, then it's time to seriously examine both your standards and your self-esteem. As I've said before, whatever good and wonderful and desirable experience this life allows, *you are worth it*, and I want you to go out and get it now. Settle for more, girlfriend. Settle for more.

The problem often is we talk about "being alone" in tones

usually reserved for such things as "being on a respirator." We're particularly fond of voicing aloud our fear and dread of "dying alone." Well, unless we can get a bunch of people to commit mass suicide with us, we probably *are* going to die alone, no matter what kind of relationship we do or do not have. It's just the nature of death. (And even if for some bizarre reason you do end up dying with a bunch of other people, is that better somehow?) The point of this rant is: Quit telling yourself scary shit. It's not helping anything, and it's not even true, so just quit it.

Throughout this book, I've been carrying on about men and finding them and getting them and keeping them and deciding whether or not to kill them, and if so, how, and so on. And that's all funny and mostly true and all that, but the real truth is you are enough—just the way you are, just who you are. You are a complete entity, a whole person, right there in the skin you're in. You don't need to have a guy to be happy. Admit it: You have more fun with a gang of girlfriends than you've had on the absolute best date of your entire life. If somebody comes along who treats you right and makes you happy and you can do the same for him, well, that's just dandy. But I'm telling you, the only way that I know to get and keep a happy, healthy relationship is first to create a happy and healthy life for yourself *without* one. This is your life to live.

My friend Sarah Ellen McDonald (the former Miss Okra!) is one of the single most talented people I know. Not only can she write and sing trashy love songs, she can dance provocatively while balancing a *full* beer on top of her head. She can also clog, tap-dance, hang Sheetrock, change tires like a tire-changing fiend, sing the alphabet backward, split firewood, play the guitar, piano, *and* banjo, trim horses' hooves, and wire your house for electricity, phone, and cable. She can also make her best friend laugh so hard that milk comes out her nose; plus, she can nearly always open jars that nobody else can. Now, I ask you, do you think this woman *settles* in relationships? She does not, nor should she—and neither should you. Will she be at loose ends if she doesn't have a man in her life for a while? I think you know the answer to that.

I've heard it said that if you keep one foot in yesterday and one foot in tomorrow, well, you just can't help but shit all over today. And today is all anybody ever has. And if you do get a tomorrow, won't it be fine to remember and be glad of what you did yesterday?

## PART V

# Food and Feeding

# 17

## Nab the Tummy — the Heart Will Be Along Directly

An absolutely precious and wise-beyond-her-years Queen in Texas sent me some sage advice about Texas men. (I have lost her e-mail and thus don't have her name, and Hunny, I apologize, but your advice is way too important to the women of the world to withhold on a technicality.) This ultimate Yellow Rose of Texas wrote me that, in order to get and keep a Texas man, you must be able to fuck and fry meat—and you must be willing and able to do it on a pretty regular basis. Furthermore, if you ever decide that you want to be *rid* of the man, you must be willing to quit fucking and frying meat. That's the only way to run 'em off over there in Texas. And don't you know that's the truth everywhere. If you just quit the fucking but keep on frying, he'll get the sex elsewhere and come on back to eat your cooking. Likewise, if you reverse your offerings, he'll just grab something from the Whattaburger and show up at home for "dessert." Only when there is absolutely nothing waiting for him at home will he just go on off and leave you be. I imagine that this is pretty much true no matter what part of the country you're from; only the requisite food would change.

Here is some good news for you in the fuck-and-fry-meat department: We all know that frying can be a tedious, often nearly thankless chore, which too often renders one simply not in the mood for the other part of the deal, and we certainly don't want *that* part to become a chore. With that in mind and in keeping with our Official Sweet Potato Queens Policy, "Never wear panties to a party," we are now offering, for your gustatory and partying pleasure, not one but two new Official Sweet Potato Queens beverages, made especially for us by W. Park Kerr, one of *the* absolute cutest men in the world and owner of the fabulous El Paso Chili Company. These may be used alternately and intermittently to achieve the desired results of the moment. These liquid wonders of the world are none other than the Sweet Potato Queens' Panty-Remover™ Margaritas and the Sweet Potato Queens' Ruby Red ReVirginator™ Margaritas. You can easily see how you would use the first one for a while—until you need the second one, and then you use that until you're ready to start over, and so on and so forth. We consider these drink mixes another of our many and varied and tireless contributions toward World Peace—not to be confused with Whirled Peas, for which we do offer a recipe in this section. (You'll find the drink mixes in our store at sweetpotatoqueens.com.) And now—drink in hand— let the meat frying begin!

## *Meat and 'Maters*

If you're not in the mood to fry on a given evening but are nonetheless inclined to feed him a little something—just because you're such an uncommonly sweet and good-natured woman—then here's a meat thing to try: Get about **3½ pounds of round steak** and cut little pockets in it, lengthwise, and stick **a piece of bacon** in each of the pockets. Combine **¼ teaspoon each of black pepper, red pepper, and salt** and smear that on the outside of the meat. Melt **⅓ cup of butter** in a skillet (black iron would be good) and brown the meat on both sides in that. Then add **1½ tablespoons of dark brown sugar, 3 cups of canned tomatoes** (or, if it's summertime and you have fabulous home-grown 'maters and you are truly an uncommonly sweet and good-natured woman, you could cook up some real ones— wouldn't *that* be just too good for most men we know?), and **1¼ cups water.** Put all that in there with the meat, cover the pan, turn the heat way, way down, and just let it simmer for about an hour and a half, or until the meat is tender.

## *Manly, Meatly Squash*

This is also not fried, and a bit of a pain in the ass to make, but I think you will like it so much your ownself that you'll find it well worth the trouble. You're gonna be using yellow (summer) squash, rice, and ground beef, and you'll use your own judgment as to how much of each, depending on how much of it you want to make. I recommend making a bunch. The basic recipe is this: Cut **3 big yellow squash** in half, lengthwise, and scrape out the guts. Put **2 cups of water** and **1 teaspoon of salt** in a big pot with a lid and bring it to a boil. Then add the squash, cut side down, and cook 'em over medium heat for about 5 minutes, or until they get tender. Then take the squash out and set them on paper towels to drain. Heat up about **1 tablespoon of bacon drippings** in an iron skillet (if you've got it) and throw in some **garlic** and about **½ pound of ground beef** (nothing too fatty) and cook it until the meat's brown. Then add about **½ cup of uncooked white rice, 1 teaspoon salt, ½ teaspoon pepper,** and **2 cups of stewed tomatoes.** Cover that and cook it over low heat until the liquid is absorbed; this should take about 20 minutes. Have a Sweet Potato Queens' Panty-Remover Margarita (again, available only from us at sweetpotatoqueens.com) while that's cooking.

And while you're getting sauced, you can make the sauce for this dish. Melt **2 tablespoons of butter** in a pan and add **2 tablespoons flour, ½ teaspoon dry mustard, ¼ teaspoon salt, ¼ teaspoon red pepper,** and **1 cup milk.** Cook that until it gets thick; then turn the heat down and add at least ¼ **cup sharp Cheddar cheese** and cook it until the cheese melts. Take your little squashes and fill 'em up with the meat mixture. Then place them in a baking dish, pour half the sauce over them, and bake at 350 degrees for about 15 to 20 minutes. Before you eat them, pour on the rest of the sauce.

## *Tammy Donna's Kay~So Dip*

Yes, it sounds sort of like the more usual *queso*, except that Tammy Donna is from Magee, Mississippi, and they don't spell stuff with *q*'s and pronounce it like *k*'s in Magee, Mississippi. *Queso* would be pronounced "quee-zo" down there in Simpson County. And if you spell it "kay-so," the *a* can be a much longer sound, which Tammy Donna prefers, naturally. But yes, it does involve massive amounts of cheese. Just because this recipe is attributed to Tammy Donna, you should in no way construe from that that she does, ever has, or ever will actually make it. She merely likes to *eat* it after someone else—anyone, she's not picky about that—has made it. And this recipe serves only one if Tammy Donna is in the crowd, so take that into account if she's in the vicinity.

Okay, get a double boiler and commence boiling some water in the bottom of it. Then turn the heat way down, and in the top part put **1 pound of shredded white cheese** (just the right amount, yes?). This could be Pepper Jack—always good—or it could be Manchego—yum yum *yum*. Slowly melt that "kay-so," giving it a little whisk every now and then to show it you love it and are paying attention to it. When it's melted, add **a big red bell pepper,** chopped up real fine, some uncooked **fresh spinach leaves** (suit your own taste as to how much spinach, but remember it's gonna wilt down to just nothing when it gets hot), and **a couple of small-to-medium chopped tomatoes.** Then very slowly stir in **a quart of low-fat milk**—add a little bit every few minutes and stir it a bit; take your time and keep the heat low. This stuff is good on any kind of chip, bread, or cracker. It's also good on fingers—hell, it's probably good on dirt clods. There will be no leftovers.

## Cutest Boy in the World's Mama's Broccoli Casserole

Now, you know that every man alive has a mama and there is some dish that his mama makes that he just purely loves, and it behooves you to learn how to make it. The Cutest Boy in the World's mama is a bread-making fiend, and I could not hope in this life ever to replicate any of her bread. When he was in sixth grade, she would make her melt-in-your-mouth homemade cinnamon rolls, and every day for weeks he took them to school and sold them to the cinnamon-roll-starved children for a dollar each—which was a big wad of money for a grade-schooler to have back then. Unfortunately for Cutie Pie, Mama found out and punished him: She baked giant bags full of cinnamon rolls and didn't let him have *any* and made him take them to school and *give* them away to his former "customers." Is it any wonder he became a lawyer? Anyway, I cannot deal with yeast. It's just one of those things, like backing up in a car, I simply cannot do, and after enough failures, I have accepted this about myself. Can't do reverse, can't cook with yeast, can't sing—oh, the list goes on and on. But I had to find *something* that his mama makes that I could have a prayer of whipping up with my own hands in my own kitchen, and she was sweet enough to give me a real easy one.

All you do is cook **2 10-ounce packages of frozen broccoli florets** and drain them. Then sauté **1 big chopped onion** in about **½ stick of butter.** Dump the broccoli and the onions into a two-quart casserole and add **1 can of cream of mushroom soup** (YIPPEE—it's the Southern Staple!), **1 roll of garlic cheese** (they've just about quit making this stuff, so if you can't find it, just sauté some garlic with the onions and then use a bunch of regular ole shredded sharp Cheddar cheese), **a 4-ounce can of sliced mushrooms, a can of water chestnuts,** and **½ cup of toasted sliced almonds.** Stir all that up and then top it with **Ritz cracker crumbs** and **a little butter** and cook it at 350 degrees until it gets bubbly (about 30 minutes). You can double it, you can freeze it, and you cannot mess it up. I am living proof.

## The Ubiquitous Biscuit

I have yet to meet the man who does not purely love a biscuit. They want 'em all the time, with everything, and they want 'em bad. It follows, then, that they also have fond feelings for the biscuit maker, which can be *you*. I recommend making these biscuits on a regular basis for your ownself—share them with him if you're of a mind to, but it's not mandatory.

Remember when you're making biscuits, the main thing is *do not fool with the dough a whole lot;* if you do, you will get crackers, which, although tasty, are just not the same as biscuits, on account of the crunch factor. So, for these, my personal favorite biscuits, get and mix together the dry stuff—**3 cups all-purpose flour, ½ teaspoon salt, ⅓ cup sugar, 1 tablespoon baking powder,** and **½ teaspoon baking soda.** Then cut in **¾ cup of butter** until it's crumbly and add **1 cup of buttermilk,** stirring just until it's all moist. (Again, don't be beating the biscuit dough—it will turn on you, I'm telling you.) Flop the dough out onto a well-floured surface, smooth it out, and then roll it out to about ½-inch thickness and cut out little biscuits with whatever cutter you want (the one I use is about 2 inches in diameter and this makes for about 3 dozen biscuits, which, coincidentally, is just about how many I can eat at a sitting). Bake the biscuits on an ungreased cookie sheet at 400 degrees for about 13 minutes, or until they are as brown as you personally like them to be. These biscuits are every bit as good stone cold as they are hot out of the oven—pretty high praise for a biscuit. I don't know many other biscuits I can say that about.

## Beer and a Sammich

You've heard that old joke about the perfect woman, who does this, that, and the other thing, and then at midnight, she turns into a sandwich and a six-pack? Well, just tee-fuckin-hee is all I can say—except maybe for a little har-dee-har-har. We ain't goin' nowhere, buckwheat, but if you play your cards right, we just might make you this very fine sammich and bring you a beer. My good buddy Jeanie in Tonasket, Washington, told me how to make this, and if you don't salivate reading about it, you are just dried slap up is all I can say for you.

Take a slice or a slab of **sourdough bread** and **butter** it—a lot—and put it butter side down on the grill. Then lay some **provolone or Pepper Jack cheese** on top and some **roast beef slices** on top of that. Then get another hunk of sourdough and slather a bunch of really good **bleu cheese dressing** on one side of it and a bunch of **butter** on the other side and put it, bleu cheese side down, on top of the grilling sandwich. When the cheese inside looks melty, flip it over and grill it on the other side. When it's toasted on that side, slap it on a plate and try to keep from crying—just eat it.

## Bacon and Beagle Dicks

I had just barely met Queen Corinne when she got right to the heart of the matter—bacon, of course. Take **a pound of bacon,** she says to me—and I'm all ears at the sound of *those* words—

and cut the pieces into thirds. Then, says she, take **a package of Li'l Smokies cocktail sausages.** (I confess a decided fondness for the teeny weenies—despite an entire blues song about them written and performed at great length on special occasions by Rex Henderson and John Bush entitled "Beagle Dicks.") Wrap a piece of bacon around each Smokie and stick a toothpick in strategically. Line 'em all up on a cookie sheet and dump a bunch of **dark brown sugar** over 'em and bake 'em at 350 degrees until the bacon is crispy. Eat 'em while they're hot, Corinne says—a clear indication of just how recently we met. Anybody who's known me for longer than twenty minutes would know it would be a miracle if I didn't eat the whole thing—cookie sheet and all—right out of the oven.

## *There's Always Room for Bacon*

One can never have enough bacon-based appetizers on hand— truly words to live by. Queen Cindy gave me this ezy-breezy-greezy-cheezy recipe that I simply adore. All you need (for this recipe and for most of life, truth be told) is **bacon, Club or Waverly crackers,** and **Parmesan cheese.** Preheat the oven to 250 degrees—that's a low oven, not a typo; she did not mean 350. Put foil on a cookie sheet (you'll be glad you did) and cut the bacon into thirds. Put a piece of raw bacon on each cracker and put the crackers on the foil. Then just dump a bunch of Parmesan over them and bake at 250 for 2 hours. This next part is important: Take them out of the oven and *leave them alone—*

just let 'em sit there on the cookie sheet and cool off completely, and don't touch 'em until they do. This cooling-off period allows for maximum re-absorption of any grease that may have inadvertently escaped during baking. If you leave them alone until they are stone cold, they will be crispy and wonderful. Don't refrigerate them; put them in Tupperware—assuming that you don't eat every single one of them on the spot, of course.

## Armadillo Tails

As with our yummy Armadillo Dip from *The Sweet Potato Queens' Book of Love*, no armadilli are harmed in the making of this dish. Queen Kristin gave me this recipe, and we love her for that. Get **a whole bunch of fresh jalapeño peppers.** Then put on rubber gloves and I'm not kidding—if you don't, you will be sixty kinds of sorry. Gloved, cut the peppers in half, lengthwise, and remove the seeds and ribby stuff, and set them aside—we'll get back to them in a minute. Now, either brown and cut up boneless **chicken breast** or just buy the kind that's already been grilled and cut up (my pick). Microwave some **cream cheese** on low until it gets soft and stir some **chili powder** into it until it's a nice pale orange color. Overstuff each jalapeño half with the orange cream cheese and put some chicken on there, then— YIPPEE—wrap the whole thing in—what else?—**bacon!** Then stick a toothpick in to hold it. This is why we say to overstuff with cheese—it's gonna squish out when you stick the toothpick in, and you want to allow for that and not be suffering from cream cheese shortage later on. Then you grill 'em until the bacon's done enough for your taste. I recommend putting them in one of those little grill basket contraptions where you put the food in and close the top and then you just flip the whole basket over when the food has grilled long enough on one side—instead of laboriously trying to flip over ten thousand little drippy, cheesy hunks of peppers and bacon.

Caution: If you put this in your mouth the second it comes off the grill (which you will want to do), I promise you, there will be not a trace of hide left on your entire tongue, and for the next month, you can eat dog shit and not taste it. Cream cheese gets hotter than molten lava—this is a scientific fact, proven and demonstrated repeatedly by countless and wildly expensive government studies paid for with your hard-earned tax dollars.

## Whirled Peas

Often confused with "world peace" and nearly as desirable. You can make this with fresh or frozen green peas. When we were growing up we called them English peas, but I don't see that on any labels anywhere—only "green"—so I don't know if we made that up or what, but they are not black-eyed, purple hull, or crowder peas, I can tell you that for a fact. They're little and green, and the ones in the can should be outlawed. Anyway, melt **a stick of butter** in a big skillet and throw in **a bunch of thin-sliced carrots** (if you want thicker slices of carrots, cook the carrots for a few minutes in the microwave first so they don't take six months to get soft) and **a bunch of green peas.** Cook these for a few minutes until the carrots get soft and then throw in **a bunch of chopped fresh dill.** In my opinion, you can't put too much dill in there, but suit yourself. Cook it for a few more minutes and then eat it all straight out of the skillet.

## Nana's Sacred Matzo Ball Soup

You say he's a nice Jewish boy? Ah! We should all be so lucky! But what to feed such a one? Not to worry. My precious Jeffrey Gross has given us his Nana's Sacred Matzo Ball Soup recipe, which he got from his ever-gracious Aunt Diane. Aunt Diane swears it is very easy, but time-consuming, so you must have patience. Well, I love matzo ball soup, so for this, I'm willing to try to cultivate some patience. Aunt Diane (and Nana before her) says to use *only* Manischewitz Matzo Meal; anything else will have an undesirable texture. So fine—we'll use it. So you want **½ cup of matzo meal, 2 large beaten eggs, 1 teaspoon of salt,** and **2 tablespoons of chicken fat.** According to Aunt Diane (and Nana before her), there is no substitute for chicken fat (I myself can't think of one), and so you must ask a butcher to give you some. Once you've got your chicken fat, you've got to heat it in a pan, so if there's anything funky in it besides the pure fat itself, it will separate from the fat itself. Then you strain it through a paper towel or cheesecloth and refrigerate it until it congeals again. Clearly, we can tell already just from this huge Chicken Fat Errand that this Matzo Ball Soup thing is just a big-ass deal—but it's gonna be worth it, I promise. You'll love it and your Jewish boyfriend will just *plotz!*

Okay, we've done all this preliminary crap to the chicken fat. So you've got your matzo meal, your eggs, your salt, and your chicken fat, and you mix all that together and then you add **2 tablespoons of chicken broth** (this may be canned, thank you very much, Aunt Diane—and Nana before her), and mix it up. Then you cover it and put it in the refrigerator until it solidifies and is easy to shape into 1-inch balls (about 20 minutes).

Next boil about **1½ quarts of water** (it should be boiling "briskly"), then reduce the heat to low and drop your matzo balls in. Cover the pot and let it boil for 40 to 60 minutes. Aunt Diane (and Nana before her) says that the balls will swell up considerably as they boil, so you want to make sure that there's plenty of water and not an overload of balls in the pot. (There's a further life lesson in there somewhere, I'm sure.) Before removing the balls, make sure to very gently test them with a fork to see that they are soft all the way through. If they are not, you must keep adding water and boiling until they are. Patience! Aunt Diane (and Nana before her) says she gets about five balls out of this mixture and she usually has four pots of water going at the same time, using the entire one-pound box of Matzo Meal and making gazillions at one time and freezing the whole deal. I guess so—you wouldn't want to be whipping this up from scratch every weekend, that's for sure.

Now, when the balls come out of the boiling water, they should be going directly into the chicken soup so they can absorb the flavor. So you will have previously made chicken soup according to the following recipe! (I hope you are still in love with that Jewish boy by this time; he is a *lot* of trouble, and he'd better make it worth your while!)

The chicken soup is from Jeffrey's mom. So before you make the matzo balls, do this: Cut up **a whole chicken** and put it in about **a gallon of water** with at least **3 cloves of garlic, 2 teaspoons of salt, a big onion cut in quarters, 4 or so big carrots cut in 1-inch slices, 2 stalks of celery cut in 1-inch slices, a bunch of parsley,** and **a bunch of dill.** Cook all that until the chicken gets done. Remove the chicken and shred the meat, discarding the bones, fat, and skin. Strain the chicken broth, then taste it, and if it's not "strong" enough for your taste (chicken soup is a very personal thing), add some chicken bouillon. Put the chicken back in the broth—get it all hot and ready for the matzo balls when they come out of the boiling water.

Mercy! What a lot of trouble! I can tell you, though, it is the Ultimate Comfort Food and you will love it your ownself—even if you don't have a Jewish boyfriend. (Hint: If you live in or go to New York City, go to the diner in the Edison Hotel and you can get this brought straight to your table, with no work whatsoever on your part. I wonder if they would consider overnighting me some?)

## Better'n His Own Mama's Chicken and Dumplins

I haven't met too many Southern boys who don't love chicken and dumplins—and the few who don't are highly suspect. Queen Diana knows about feeding happy Southern boys and she says do this: Get a big pot and cook **a big chopped onion, 3 thinly sliced carrots,** and **4 stalks of coarsely chopped celery** in **a few tablespoons of canola oil** until they get tender. Then throw in **3 cups of chicken chunks,** some **black pepper** (if you like it—I don't), and **6 cups of chicken broth.** Turn the heat down and simmer it for about 15 to 20 minutes. Meanwhile, put **1½ cups of self-rising flour** in a bowl and cut in **¼ shortening** until the mixture is like crumbs. Add **2 tablespoons of chopped fresh parsley** and **½ cup chicken broth** and stir just until it's all moistened. Then drop that dough by the tablespoon into the simmering chicken stuff, cover the pot, and *do not peek* while it cooks for the next 15 minutes. (It's like taking the cover off when rice is cooking—very bad juju. Don't do it.)

## Queen Esther's Yam Delight

If you are an author with a big publishing house and they like your book, they will send you on a book tour, and if they not only like your book but they like *you,* then they will arrange for Esther Levine to be your media escort in Atlanta. Esther is just the Queen of Atlanta. She knows everything and everybody worth knowing in the entire city, and she will make your author's life worth living while you are entrusted to her care. I am honored that my esteemed and very cute publishers have always made certain that I have my time with Esther on each book tour. I quake at the thought of one day arriving at the Atlanta airport to find that Esther is not there. I shall shut down my computer and write no more from that day forward.

On my last trip to Esther's Queendom, she gave me this great sweet 'tater pie recipe, knowing my weakness not only for sweet 'taters but for pies as well. Start by preheating the oven to 350 degrees. Then mix together **1 cup all-purpose flour, ¼ cup powdered sugar, ⅓ cup chopped pecans,** and **7 tablespoons butter,** and press all that into the bottom of a 13 × 9 × 2-inch baking pan and bake it for 20 minutes and then set it aside to cool. Then mix together **1 8-ounce package of softened cream cheese** and **⅔ cup powdered sugar** until it's all creamy. Then fold in **¾ cup Cool Whip.** (God love her, Esther says we can use fat-free cream cheese and fat-free **Cool Whip**—tee-hee!) Spread the cream cheese mixture over the cooled crust. In another bowl, mix together **1 29-ounce can of drained sweet potatoes, ¼ cup sugar,** and **¼ teaspoon cinnamon** and spread that over the cream cheese stuff. Top with **Cool Whip,** sprinkle some **chopped pecans** over that, and refrigerate. Yam-yum.

## *Turtle Pie*

Again, as with the armadillos, I must assure you that Queen
Leslie assured me that no turtles will be harmed in the making
of this pie. You will, however, be slower than an armadillo if you
eat much of this, on account of you will be fat, fat, fat. But you'll
be happy, happy, happy—so fine. Start by crumbling a bunch of
Oreos to make **1½ cups of Oreo cookie crumbs.** (Now for me,
if I need to end up with a cup and a half of crumbs, I'm gonna
have to start with about a bushel of Oreos, but you may have a
tad more self-restraint, although the fact that you've read this
far in this book leads me to suspect otherwise.) At any rate, get
your Oreo crumbs and stir them up with **⅓ cup of melted butter** and mash all that into a deep-dish 9-inch pie plate and freeze
it for 15 minutes. (I'm not sure there's any reason to do this
freezing part other than to get it away from your mouth long
enough to make the rest of the pie, but do it anyway, just in
case.) If you are just a hopeless, lazy slackass, or you simply
cannot quit eating the Oreos long enough to get the crumbs
made, you can buy a ready-made chocolate piecrust. Then put
**1¼ cups semisweet Nestlé's chocolate chips, 1 cup evaporated
(*not* condensed) milk,** and **1 cup mini-marshmallows** in a heavy
pot and cook it over low heat, stirring constantly, getting high
on the fumes, until it's thick and smooth. Then set it aside
to cool. Spread **2 cups of high-quality vanilla ice cream**
(Mississippi girls prefer Luvel, naturally) into the cooled Oreo
crust, and cover and freeze for 30 minutes. Then pour half the

chocolate mixture over the ice cream, cover, and freeze for another 30 minutes. Then lay down another layer of ice cream and freeze. Then another layer of chocolate and freeze again. Then put **16 toasted pecan halves** on the top layer and kinda press 'em down into the chocolate. Serve with a bucket of **caramel sauce**—and only to people you like a lot.

## *Jim Frye's Sacred Dessert Recipe*

Here we've been slaving in the kitchen forever, and who should turn up but one of our very favorite Spud Studs, from Hawaii (Ha-war-ya around here), saying how much he loves the Sweet Potato Queens philosophies, and to prove it he was giving us this recipe. It would prove his devotion a damn sight better if he would come over here and *make* it for us, but we think his heart is in the right place—even if it is in the middle of the ocean over there. If Jim were here with us now, he would get a big skillet and throw in equal parts, say, about **4 or 5 tablespoons** each of **butter** and **dark brown sugar** (we love him, yes?), and then when that has melted satisfactorily, he would throw in **a tablespoon or so of lemon juice** and about **4 tablespoons of orange juice** and then he'd add **a bunch of fresh sliced strawberries** to the mix. While that's cooking down a bit and getting all slurpy and wonderful, we'd be drinking the Panty-Remover Margarita he made for us, then he would dish up a big bowlful of **vanilla ice cream** and pour them berries right on top of it. (He could add some **Grand Marnier** and set it on fire, but he feels that's a waste of perfectly good booze and we are inclined to agree.)

## *Butterfinger Cake*

Queen Sandra Howley sent me a recipe with the caveat that it may be too good to share. Here it is, so you can see for yourself. Make a **butter-in-it yellow cake mix** according to the package directions—except add a **running-over teaspoon of vanilla** to it. While that's baking, mix up the filling—which is **3 (three!) 8-ounce packs of Philadelphia Cream Cheese** (you could use the low- or nonfat varieties or a combination thereof if you were "thinking thin"—*ha!*), **3 (three!) cans of Eagle Brand Sweetened Condensed Milk** (again, you could use nonfat), and **1 very large container of Cool Whip** (and this comes in nonfat, too). Okay, stir all that up together and put it somewhere out of reach so you don't eat it all while you're doing this other stuff. Get about a ton of Butterfingers—really, **3 14-ounce bags of baby Butterfingers** (that's right at three pounds of Butterfingers—is this obscene or what?). You either chop up the Butterfingers or give 'em a whirl in the Cuisinart, and after you've done that—again, put them somewhere out of reach for a few minutes.

When the cake is done and has cooled off, cut it up into little pieces and line a bowl with a layer of 'em, then slather those cake pieces with a thick layer of the filling and put half the Butterfinger bits on top of that. Repeat and then take the phone off the hook and lock the doors and get a big spoon and have at it. Now, when I made this, by those instructions, I had a whole bunch of the filling stuff left over—even after I ate a bunch of it, and even though I gobbed it on the cake layers really thick. So you can either freeze the extra (enough for about a half recipe the next time) or you can cut the filling ingredients by a third or you can just stand there and eat all the leftovers. I'd opt for the latter because it's just free eating—it doesn't count as calories because it's left over and you're eating it straight out of the bowl it was mixed in; you'd be crazy to pass up this opportunity.

This reminds me of an incident with a cake from many, many years ago. My best friend, Alice Ann, and I were out with a bunch of our pseudohippie buddies, and by and by, as would happen back then, we got the munchies. Like locusts, we devoured everything in our immediate vicinity, but then Alice Ann and I remembered that we had bought and put in her freezer that very afternoon a very large Sara Lee Pecan Coffee Cake, and it got to calling us real loud. So we commenced to nagging everybody there to take us back to Alice Ann's so we could eat that very large Sara Lee Pecan Coffee Cake. After a time, we were successful in getting everybody piled back in the van for the ride back to Alice Ann's. (Remember when it was cool to have a van? I swear, kids today do not know what they are missing here, but as the mother of a teenage daughter, I can tell you, I am thrilled that vans have become the sole domain of soccer moms.)

Anyway, we got back to Alice Ann's and everybody was laid out all over the living room in a literal fog, listening to Little Feat on the stereo and having what they imagined to be deep and meaningful conversations about their nineteen-year-old selves. Meanwhile, Alice Ann and I betook ourselves to the kitchen, where we retrieved Sara Lee from her frosty refuge, carefully removed her cover—replacing any loose pecans that may have stuck to the lid—and lovingly coated her with about a stick of butter before popping her into the oven to warm. Christmas has never been slower than Sara Lee was that night, but finally she was hot—her pecans toasted, her icing melted, her butter oozing delightfully into her every crevice. We lifted her reverently from the oven and placed her gently on the kitchen floor between us, where we sat, forks in hand. As soon as the butter stopped sizzling, we pounced on her, and in a flurry of forks, she was gone. We were inordinately happy.

At that precise moment, the kitchen door swung open and one of the crew from the living room lurched in, inquiring as to the whereabouts of the cake they'd heard so much about. As soon as we informed him, dismissively, that we had eaten it all, it dawned on us: In our whining and wheedling for a ride to the apartment to commune with Sara Lee, they had somehow gotten the idea that they would be sharing in that experience. Let me tell you, *that* had never occurred to us! We never had any intention whatsoever of giving anybody else so much as a crumb of that cake. And, in truth, we never implied such a thing. All we said was "Hey, man, take us back to the apartment; we want to eat a coffee cake." And they did and we did and that was that. The Sara Lee episode occurred more than thirty years ago, and Alice Ann and I can still get hysterical over the expressions on their faces when they realized that we had eaten that whole cake—and they were stupid enough to have expected otherwise.

All I'm saying is, when you sit down with your Butterfinger Cake, precedent has been set.

# THE LAST WORD

## When It's Good, It's Very, Very Good!

We've talked plenty about what a relationship is like when it's horrid, but what about when the planets do align and nobody turns out to be an ax murderer, including you? Does it happen? Have you ever seen it? In my life, I've been fortunate to see what I believe to be a few Great Loves: my parents, for example, and JoAnne and Willie Morris, Gayle and John Christopher, Joan and Buster Bailey, Billie Sue and Bill Jennings, Gail and John Pittman, Cynthia and Joe Speetjens, Allen Payne and Jeffrey Gross, Cindy and Johnny Glass, and Allie and Roy Hyde. These are couples I've known personally who have something that feels warm and good when you're in the room with them. It is something worth having, enviable even.

To love and be loved is surely the greatest joy on earth. It's also the greatest show on earth for everyone in the vicinity of lovers and their beloved. Whether the love is that of a young couple drunk with newfound infatuation or an old couple sated by a lifetime of loving each other or a little boy holding his first wriggling puppy in his arms as he flashes a heart-stopping grin at his adoring mother as she takes his picture—all make you smile clean through your soul. Just being in the presence of genuine love is truly a tender mercy in this life. The finest example I know of Love at Its Best happened when I was in the courtyard of a hotel in New Orleans. It must have been early spring, since heat, humidity, rain, and/or mosquitoes ruled out courtyard lounging pretty much any other time of the year. I was alone having coffee and mouth-breathing. Across the way, a large group of folks, probably gathered for a family reunion, were laughing and talking, but after a bit, they all left except a little bitty girl in a stroller, about a year old, and a very old man—probably her great-grandfather. He was standing behind her, leaning over, looking at her face reflected in the glass doors of the patio. He was stroking her little head, gently lifting the wisps of her pale gold silky hair. His touch was so light, it wouldn't have disturbed a dandelion puff. She was perfectly still, gazing back at the reflection of his wrinkled old face and faded eyes, which were so completely and nakedly filled with the overwhelming love he felt for this precious child. Neither of them made a sound. Both were completely unaware of anything but each other. It was a moment of perfect holiness. I was struck dumb by the power of it. So much was spoken in that silent space.

The very old man, lovingly touching the perfect head of this tiny child, was remembering, I suspect, the silky hair of his own baby daughter, and her daughter's after that, and now, to be granted the great gift of loving yet another baby girl in his long life, he was obviously overcome with love and gratitude. Perhaps, in the far reaches of his memory, lived the sweet recollection of his own father touching his own little baby head with such love and reverence. He had to know the fragility and impermanence of the moment—that this child would probably be the last of the babies in his life, and that the times left to stroke the head of this one were numbered, and counting down more rapidly than he could bear. But at that very moment, all was well with his soul, and he was perfectly happy and at peace.

She, the precious infant, was simply alive in the moment, loving it, receiving it—completely unconscious of life and the pain it brings on occasion to us all. I wondered—and I wondered if the old man wondered—if she would have any real memory of this moment as she grew up. Would she be able, in times of fear or sorrow, to call up the image I saw before me that day? The sweet warm air of the courtyard, the little baby, and the very old man, loving and being loved in perfect harmony and completeness. Would she know—regardless of what fate would bring her way in life—would she know that at least one time in her life, she was utterly loved by another human being? You know, sometimes just that little bit of knowledge is all we have to carry us through, all we have to cling to—and it can be all we need.

When the others in the family reappeared in the courtyard, I was sitting there with tears streaming down my face—as they are now as I write this. I went over to the group and took the women aside—the mother, the grandmother, the great-grandmother—and I told them, through my tears, what I had witnessed. Take their picture right this minute, in this very spot, I told them. Promise me you'll show her this picture and tell her the story of this day, and that you'll never let her forget him and his love for her and this perfect moment in her little life. No one knows what life has in store for her, or who among you will be here when she needs you, I said, but she will forever have this day to remind her of how much she was loved. We all cried, and as I left, they were taking the photograph.

When love is good and right, I believe, it's the way God loves us—beyond all reason—and it not only blesses the lives of the lovers themselves but everyone around them. May we all experience such love in our lives, and may we recognize it and treasure it every second.

## ACKNOWLEDGMENTS

As far as I know, I am the world's *only* full-time professional Sweet Potato Queen, and although I did put myself squarely on this throne, it does take about a gajillion people to help keep me on it, and I would like to thank them—and give them each a pony. The thanks are below—the pony's in the mail.

Jenny Frost, Steve Ross, Philip Patrick, Rachel Kahan, Brian Belfiglio, Lindsay Mergens, Linda Kaplan, Alex Lencicki, David Tran, Amy Boorstein, Camille Smith, and Lauren Dong—the lovely and amazing crew at Crown/Three Rivers, without whom I would still be the Sweet Potato Queen—but hardly anybody would know it.

Stephen Wallace at Random House and the folks who make him look good—Eileen Becker, Warren Bost, Karen Hayes, Toni Hetzel, Julie Kurland, and Chuck Errig.

If JoAnne Prichard Morris ever gets tired of fooling with me, I guess I'll have to quit writing—I can't imagine a more talented

# Acknowledgments

editor, and certainly not a more patient one. My work requires large amounts of both from an editor, I'm afraid.

My precious darlin' agent, Jenny Bent, and all the folks at Trident Media Group for making sure I can pay the light bill and Bailey's tuition.

Donna Kennedy Sones, for Queenly vision and Saintly patience. Sara Babin and Alycia Jones for keeping the Web site between the ditches.

Malcolm White for putting on the best parade in the country every year—no matter what. And Hal White and Charly Abraham and Anne Friday at Hal & Mal's for making all the Queens feel so welcome every year.

The entire staff of the Jackson Hilton—our new and very happy home for Parade Week.

Katherine Gilmore Callahan—little Larva Queen—for staring down her college administrator and duct-taping her tiara on to her mortarboard for graduation—and becoming the most amazing costumer ever.

Tom and Margaret Joynt, not only for the great photos but for feeding us so well at the photo shoots.

Liza Looser for spiritual support, Rick Looser for thinking we're hot, and the entire staff of the Cirlot Agency for our award-winning logos and Web site design.

Jay Sones—I gotta say it, *bless his heart* for his apparently *boundless* patience and surpassing skill in dealing with not only the Web site but the Message Board of Love as well.

Delta Burke, the most beautiful Sweet Potato Queen ever, and her devoted Spud Stud, Gerald McRaney.

## Acknowledgments

Johnny Evans and everybody at Lemuria Books in Jackson, Mississippi—still the only bookstore I ever *really* loved.

George Ewing, the most precious, darlin' *oughta-be* Queen in the world.

My precious daughter, Bailey, for being my heart and turning out perfect—in spite of such imperfect mothering.

The Cutest Boy in the World—Kyle Jennings—and Bad Dog Management for marrying me and taking care of bidness, as well as business.

# ABOUT THE AUTHOR

JILL CONNER BROWNE is the author of the #1 *New York Times* bestseller *The Sweet Potato Queens' Big-Ass Cookbook (and Financial Planner)*, as well as the national bestsellers *The Sweet Potato Queens' Book of Love* and *God Save the Sweet Potato Queens.* She is Boss Queen of the Sweet Potato Queens of Jackson, Mississippi, and when not writing, is a sought-after inspirational speaker.

Boss Queen Jill Conner Browne has lots more to say
about Life, Love, Men, and Being Prepared.
Not to mention the glorious recipes that started it all.
Don't miss Jill's other hilarious bestsellers:

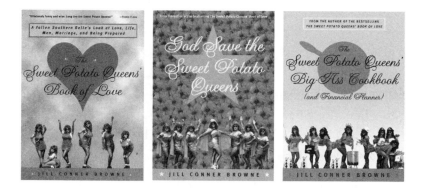

*The Sweet Potato Queens' Book of Love*

0-609-80413-8 · $13.95 paper (Canada: $21.00)

*God Save the Sweet Potato Queens*

0-609-80619-X · $13.95 paper (Canada: $21.00)

**The #1 New York Times Bestseller!**

*The Sweet Potato Queens' Big-Ass Cookbook (and Financial Planner)*

0-609-80877-X · $13.95 paper (Canada: $21.00)